Moonlighting

EARN A SECOND
INCOME AT HOME

Jo Frohbieter-Mueller

The Oasis Press®
Grants Pass, OR

Published by The Oasis Press®/PSI Research

This publication is designed to provide accurate and authoritative information in regard to the subject matter covered. It is sold with the understanding that the author and publisher are not engaged in rendering legal, accounting, or other professional service. If legal advice or other expert assistance is required, the services of a competent professional person should be sought.

— from a declaration of principles jointly adopted by a committee of the American Bar Association and a committee of publishers.

Editor: Karen Billipp
Interior design by Eliot House Productions
Cover illustration and design by Steven Burns

Please direct any comments, questions, or suggestions regarding this book to

The Oasis Press®/PSI Research:

    Editorial Department
    300 North Valley Drive
    Grants Pass, OR 97526
    (541) 479-9464
    (541) 476-1479 *fax*
    psi2@magick.net *email*

The Oasis Press® is a Registered Trademark of Publishing Services, Inc., an Oregon corporation doing business as PSI Research.

Library of Congress Cataloging-in-Publication Data
Frohbieter-Mueller, Jo.
      Moonlighting : earn a second income at home / Jo Frohbieter-Mueller.
  - 1st ed.
        p.   cm.
      Includes bibliographical references and index.
      ISBN 1-55571-406-4 (pbk.)
        1. Supplementary employment – United States.   2. Home-based
businesses – United States. I. Title.

HD5854.55.U5 F76 1997
658/.041 21
                                                                97-040968
                                                                    CIP

Printed and bound in the United States of America
First Edition 10 9 8 7 6 5 4 3 2 1 0

 Printed on recycled paper when available.

Table of Contents

A comprehensive list of nearly 500 occupations along with resource books that can be operated out of a home. Special emphasis is given to occupations that work nicely as secondary vocations.

Publications and associations of values to home workers.

Dedication

This book is dedicated to the memory of my beloved husband, Dr. Wayne P. Mueller.

Preface

THERE IS MORE TO LIFE THAN WORKING FOR SOMEONE ELSE. I wrote this book because I discovered the joys and rewards of being my own boss. I wanted to share the adventure and teach you how to get a business underway so you, too, can experience the pleasure of working for yourself. When you start your own business, you will find that when you leave your job at the end of the day or on Friday evening and head home to your own venture, your pulse and your step will quicken.

You will discover that your own business will not only bring in extra income, but it will allow you to try your wings and do the things you have always wanted to do. It will also function as a tremendous safety net because many of today's jobs with large, impersonal corporations carry with them a frightening sense of job insecurity. If the corporate rug is pulled from under your feet, your home business may keep you from falling on your face and help keep bacon on the table.

By starting a home business while working another job, you can learn the joy of being your own boss, maximize your talents, and learn what it takes to earn a living without the risk of going hungry.

While the subject of home businesses has been covered in numerous books, no other treatment approaches the task primarily from the perspective of earning a second income at home. Part-time entrepreneurship has its own set of problems and solutions and they will be dealt with in this book.

This book includes instructions for finding the right occupation, discusses zoning ordinances, getting started, funding, finding space to house a business and finding the time to make it happen. It explains how to locate supplies and how to attract customers. It addresses marketing procedures and pricing formulas, and offers valuable tax tips for home workers. It explains simple bookkeeping methods and forms of organization. And, just as importantly, it will help you to enjoy the fruits of your labor and your new adventure.

Introduction

THE TREND TOWARD WORKING AT HOME IS gathering momentum and the total number of full- and part-time home-based businesses recently exceeded 25 million. Half of the homes in America are expected to house some type of business by the turn of the century. Many of these businesses will be operated by people who work at home full-time, but others will be managed by people who have already put in eight hours at another job. The needs and *modus operandi* of people who earn a second income at home differ from those who work full-time at home, and their special needs and circumstances are addressed in this book.

One reason people moonlight from home is because the chance of making a success of their business is very high. According to Link Resources, home-based businesses have an 85 percent survival rate over a three-year period while the average three-year survival rate for general small businesses is only 20 percent. The main reason for the difference is the protective environment and the reduced costs associated with operating from home. While businesses in commercial settings must start earning from the moment their doors open in order to cover rent, taxes, and overhead expenses, home businesses can take the time to find their niche without this kind of pressure.

Moonlighters have a huge advantage over those whose only income is from home businesses; they can support their families and their home businesses through income derived from their primary occupations as the work gets underway. This is particularly valuable because it sometimes takes a good while to get a business up and running and earning a profit. During this start-up period it is very helpful to have another source of income.

Tax breaks abound for moonlighters who work from home. Besides other deductions, the government allows them to deduct business losses from other earned income to determine their tax burden. And, the valuable home-use deduction discussed later in this book is like money in the bank.

Of course, the big disadvantage of entrepreneurial moonlighting is the limited amount of time available to devote to the second occupation. However, as you will learn, time management will ensure the wise use of time, thereby freeing more moments to make moonlighting a successful way of life.

If a single word could be used to describe home businesses, that word would be "diversity." Home workers display a wide range of interests and goals as they pursue a variety of occupations, use different sites for their operations, and enjoy flexibility in work schedules.

Several factors are enhancing home business opportunities. Today's economy is service-oriented, in contrast to a manufacturing economy of the past, and as a result, the conditions for earning income at home have never been better. Generally, service-oriented occupations require less equipment and are less place-bound than manufacturing jobs. Many service occupations do not require a store front and can be run from of a basement, garage, or kitchen table; others require little in-home space because the services are provided in the customer's home or place of business. Also, the trend in the business world is for corporations to downsize, and they are relying more on subcontractors to fulfill their needs, many of whom are moonlighters working from home.

The increasing role ideas and information play in the economy and the ease with which information can be transmitted is contributing to the work-at-home, second-income movement. Computers, modems, fax machines, and other products of modern technology have made working at home a viable alternative to working in the commercial sector. Many of the jobs performed on this equipment can be done long after the lights have gone out in commercial buildings.

Retailing has also tapped into the information-moving technology, allowing this industry to find its way into our spare rooms and spare moments. Catalog sales and telemarketing are making inroads into the retailing business and both can be done just as easily at home as in commercial space. About 20 percent, or $156 billion, of all consumer purchases are spent on mail-order purchases each year, which means that approximately $3 billion worth of products are sold by mail each week. Many of these sales are made by people working at home in the evening.

Home is an especially good setting for creative work. The resurgence of interest in art and high-quality handcrafted items is attracting people to home businesses. And, freelance writing, traditionally a home business, has become one of the leading cottage industries. It is an ideal second-income business.

As long as your home business is a second job, it will probably be a part-time operation. Remember, you will spend approximately eight hours each weekday working another job, so the work you do at home must be such that it can be accomplished in a limited amount of time.

Perhaps you wonder if there really is enough time to successfully run a business at home after working elsewhere throughout the day. Even though you will be busy, you can do it if you learn to use time wisely. Some years ago I did a survey of college graduates to learn how much time they devoted to reading, watching television, and various other activities within the home. I was shocked, not only by how little time was spent reading, but that some were squandering six to seven hours each day watching television! Some respondents said they watched television because they didn't have much else to occupy their time. Unless they are exhausted from their day's work, these people could get a business up and running *As the World Turns*.

Spending time watching television or in any other non-business activity will thwart your chances of business success because ideas won't work unless you do. Most of your time at home will need to be devoted to your business if you are to be successful. For this reason, you must think about the commitment a secondary business requires and make sure you are willing to put forth the time and effort needed for such a project. You should also realize you will have less time to spend with family and friends as you strive to develop a successful business.

Even though you might think of your new business as a secondary or part-time affair, initially you will probably find yourself working harder and longer at it than at your primary job. Still, the fact remains, if you pursue a second occupation you will probably have less time to devote to it than those whose home business is their sole occupation, and you should plan your business accordingly.

As you look closely at the many kinds of secondary occupations you might undertake at home, you will discover some will complement the work you do away from home. If your day job requires mental but little physical labor, you might look for a more physical outlet for your secondary occupation; or, if you must spend days around numbing noise and a lot of activity, you may prefer more serene work at home. On the other hand, it may be wise to use the skills you use during the day to build your second-income business — just make certain to avoid any conflict of interest so your day job isn't jeopardized as a result of your home business.

The time for earning a second income at home is now. You will find the information needed to get underway in this book. Study each chapter, give your options some thought, then set your plan in motion. Don't wait for the perfect moment or until everything is in place before getting started because that may never happen. Instead, go ahead with the resources and equipment you have, make a few mistakes along the way, and discover what it takes to make your business materialize. You will find your life changed the moment you make the decision to stop thinking about it and start making your moonlighting business a reality.

Selecting the Right Business

The first objective, as you consider moonlighting at home, is finding a business that will fill your needs — one you will enjoy doing and one that will yield a profit. Part One will guide you through this process and help you select a business that is right for you.

Factors Influencing the Type of Business You Undertake

WHY DO YOU WANT TO MOONLIGHT AT HOME, and how will your special circumstances influence the type of business you select? This chapter will discuss some factors to consider in the selection process.

Take a look in and around yourself and your home and consider the following questions.

> Why do you want to work a second job at home?

> How much income is required to fill your needs, and what is the earning potential of various occupations?

> How much time can you devote to your home business, and when is the time available?

> How much, and what kind of space is available for your home business?

> What job skills, experiences, hobbies, and special interests can be used to build your business?

> What business can you build by using the equipment, tools, or vehicles you own?

> Can the location of your home be used to attract business?

> What kind of work do you enjoy?

Reasons for Starting a Home Business

People turn to moonlighting at home for five basic reasons. Supplementing income is a powerful motivator and is the prime reason most people moonlight. Working at home will enable you to bring in additional income. Maybe your primary job will keep the creditors at bay, but with today's economy and social expectations, you may find yourself working harder just to keep up. While you may not need to mortgage your home to purchase shoes for the kids, it takes a lot of money to support a family. If you want to provide a little extra, save for your children's education or for a more comfortable retirement, one job might not do the trick. Or, if you're among the 30 percent of American workers who work part-time, you may need another source of income just to meet basic needs. A second job and a second income at home could fill the gap.

Others use a second occupation as an outlet for their energy. It's true that some people come home from work exhausted, but others can hardly wait to get home to get on with their next adventure. These are the people who plant gardens, drive race cars, climb mountains, and volunteer for awesome tasks, all because they have energy to burn. A home business is one way to convert energy into accomplishments and cash; it is a way to use extra energy to add a new dimension to your life.

Another reason people strive to earn a second income at home is to prepare for retirement or a career change. Being prepared is the key to a successful retirement, whether the time is to be spent in pursuit of a golf ball, highball, or a totally new game that the retiree invents. More often than not, the new game is a business that calls on skills and talents that have been developed throughout his or her working life.

Others start home businesses while working elsewhere because their jobs are less than secure, and moonlighting is a good way to safeguard against unemployment. Their goal is to get a business underway and money coming in by the time their other job becomes history. According to the American Home Business Association, while Fortune 500 companies have eliminated over five million workers over the past decade, home-based businesses have grown during that same period and are the growth generators in today's economy.

It's wise to take advantage of the time while working elsewhere to get a business underway. The primary job not only provides security, but it also enables you to make contacts, learn skills, test wings, and make a few mistakes before being cut off from a steady job and a regular paycheck. Fifty percent of home businesses that start as part-time operations become full-time businesses.

Women who anticipate raising children find moonlighting at home to be an especially appealing way to prepare for the time when they must balance their work and their children's needs. According to a survey undertaken by the Small Business Administration, women with young children are more likely to work from home than those without young children.

Another reason people work at home is because, well — "See, I've got this idea . . . ." Ideas are the foundation of many successful businesses. Ideas lift us from the humdrum and enable us to explore uncharted territory. If you have an idea, use the fervor it generates to spur yourself to greater accomplishments. People with ideas are people with vitality, purpose, excitement; to act on an idea is to defy the limitations society inflicts on its members and allows our culture to continue to evolve. Plant a seed and a tree grows; plant an idea and a business — or humanity — grows.

Some of the most successful businesses have been built on new ideas — from sending messages through wire, which gave rise to the telephone — to making computers that converted Apples into megabucks. Most ideas don't have such widespread applications as those mentioned but they can still yield successful businesses. The intermittent windshield wiper, zipper, Velcro, Barbie doll, and hula hoop all started with ideas and yielded high profits for their inventors and developers.

If you have an idea for a business and can figure out how to convert that idea into a profit-making venture, your horizons and pocketbook will be expanded.

Generating Income

On average, home business owners earn more than those employed outside the home. According to a survey by AT&T, the average home-based entrepreneur earns $50,000 per year, while the average U.S. employee earns $26,000. About 20 percent of all home businesses earn in excess of $75,000 per year.

The earning capacity of a business is an important factor to consider. Some jobs are more profitable than others, and all business opportunities are not created equal. Some businesses yield only a modest profit, no matter how hard you work or how well you do your job, while others have the potential to produce a substantial profit. It only makes sense to "follow the money" and pursue a business that is likely to earn more rather than less.

Evaluate the earning potential of different types of businesses, and only pursue a business that has the capacity to earn a reasonable profit. Be skeptical about advertisements that offer business secrets and outlandish promises of success for a hefty fee; it takes very little common sense to separate fantasy from reality.

What are some of the better paying occupations? A few general rules can be applied. First, if you are selling something, sell bigger rather than smaller ticket items. For example, the profit a realtor earns by selling a piece of real estate can run into thousands of dollars, while the profit a neighborhood vendor earns selling ice cream on a stick is less than a dime. But it's true, if the vendor sells enough ice cream, he or she can buy the ice cream factory.

Business-to-business and business-to-government sales and services usually yield more profit than business-to-individual sales and services because businesses and the government will usually pay more than an individual for essentially the same product or service. Occupations that require more training and are performed while wearing business dress usually generate more income than those that require little training and are performed wearing work clothes, but there are surely exceptions to this rule. For instance, have you paid for the services of a painter or an electrician lately? Skills based on modern technology and using no more energy than that required to punch computer keys usually pay better than those based on back-breaking labor. Having given these guidelines, I hasten to add that there are exceptions to every one of them, and you must carefully evaluate the earning potential of each business you consider.

Never lose sight of the fact that earning money is the first goal of a business. If financial gain is not your goal, you might as well spend your spare time doing volunteer work.

Finding the Time

Generally, second-income home workers spend evenings and weekends moonlighting, thus, their home businesses must be able to function during the off hours. It would be unwise to pursue a vocation that requires meeting with business clients during the nine-to-five shift if you are involved with your primary occupation during those hours. On the other hand, many businesses can be developed during the evening hours that meet the personal needs of the nine-to-five crowd or the business needs of other moonlighters. As you study the diversity of jobs listed in the Appendix, you will find numerous occupations that can be done at night. Use Figure 1.1 to help you define the hours you will be free to moonlight.

FIGURE 1.1: Time Planner

The type and the amount of work you do will be, in part, determined by when and how much time you can devote to your business. Use the chart to outline your schedule and clarify the hours you are free to work. As you prepare this time planner, take into account your primary occupation and other responsibilities.

	Sun.	Mon.	Tues.	Wed.	Thurs.	Fri.	Sat.
4 A.M.							
5 A.M.							
6 A.M.							
7 A.M.							
8 A.M.							
9 A.M.							
10 A.M.							
11 A.M.							
NOON							
1 P.M.							
2 P.M.							
3 P.M.							
4 P.M.							
5 P.M.							
6 P.M.							
7 P.M.							
8 P.M.							
9 P.M.							
10 P.M.							
11 P.M.							
12 P.M.							
1 A.M.							
2 A.M.							
3 A.M.							

Workers whose primary jobs are seasonal often search for ways to provide continuity of income, and moonlighting at home gives them that opportunity. Home businesses are ideal for teachers who want to work during the summer months, and farmers can spend the dark winter months at another job. On the flip side of this is the person who moonlights as a farmer. Bud Meyer, of southern Indiana, was brought up on a farm and felt the need to keep his feet in the soil. His farm is located in coal mining country, and jobs in the mines pay well. Bud has figured out how to get the best of both worlds. His primary occupation is operating a huge coal mining shovel. The shovel operates around the clock, and Bud's shift runs from mid-afternoon into the night. He spends the daylight hours raising crops and cattle and tinkering with farm machinery. More important than the extra income, the farming contributes an added dimension to Bud's life. Bud's story is not uncommon because many moonlighters, fortunate enough to live on tillable land, turn the soil for extra cash.

As you read this book, you will notice the examples I have used come from the immediate area surrounding my home in southern Indiana. My neighborhood is typical of others across this nation and, if you look around your neighborhood and community, you will also find many examples of people moonlighting from home.

Finding the Space

Home businesses come in different shapes and sizes, and the kind of business you tackle will certainly be influenced by the amount and type of space you can devote to it.

In some circles the term "home business" has come to mean "home office," but this is not a true reflection of what is happening on the home front. Still, home offices are getting a lot of attention because they are perhaps the fastest growing segment of the home business phenomenon. Numerous types of businesses such as accounting, advertising, consulting, and an array of computer-oriented occupations are based on pushing papers or keys, and well-equipped offices are needed to accomplish the tasks associated with these occupations. A whole industry has emerged to meet the needs of home-based office workers, and as a result, new technology and affordable equipment has enabled them access to business opportunities that were once limited to workers in the commercial sector.

At the same time, there are people working at home who don't have anything that remotely resembles an office. At best, they might have a shoe box for bills and invoices and a small desk where they write checks and make a few phone calls. Others do office chores while sitting at the kitchen table, and they may wait for the kids to get off the line so they can make a call.

Besides the home office, a variety of locations are used by home businesses. While we tend to think they are located in or around the home, that is not always the case. Many service businesses are based at home, but the work is done off-site, frequently at the customer's location. Jobs that fit this category include construction, painting, office or house cleaning, wall papering, roofing, real estate and insurance sales, home decorating, carpet installation, and on-site maintenance and repair. On the other hand, occupations such as crafting, art work, small engine repair, mail order sales, bookkeeping and other office work, and auto repair are usually done at the home site.

Some home businesses operate out of vehicles. Trucks and vans are used when large equipment must be transported or when people or supplies must be delivered. Other successful home businesses are operated by people tooling around in cars while contacting clients through mobile phones and electronic rolodexes.

When loud or large equipment is needed to get the job done, a business might be housed in an outbuilding. Businesses that involve caring for plants or animals might grow in a field or barn, as the following story illustrates.

Last year I noticed a field at the edge of town where a cash crop was growing. I stopped to get the story and discovered "mums the word!" For the past five years Bob Dodson of Evansville, Indiana, has spent the spring and summer months planting and caring for a field of chrysanthemums. In the fall these mums are converted into cash that is being used to keep his daughter in college. Bob has turned his love of the outdoors and working with plants into a small business opportunity. His only marketing is a sign on a nearby highway that directs customers to the field of mums. Word-of-mouth has proven to be his greatest ally, and repeat customers assure that he won't get stuck with unsold plants at the end of the season. This business offers a good return on the money and energy spent, and it's a good example of how moonlighting through the wise use of space can be used to meet financial needs.

Even though many home businesses function outside the home, the fact remains that a large percentage of them are located within the home. Businesses can be found tucked into nooks and crannies and unexpected places. Some people work in their garage or basement because this is a good way to separate business life from family life; still others settle in on a side porch or spare bedroom.

Home workers who run child-care facilities often use the family room for business purposes and convert it to family use after business hours. When kitchen equipment is needed, a business might get started in the family kitchen, but since the kitchen is the heart of most homes, such a business can be intrusive and have a negative impact on family life. When a kitchen-based business starts to attract large numbers of customers, it may be necessary to move the business to an extra room or an outbuilding to accommodate the space demands.

Look around your home and think about what space can be used and how it can be converted to business use. Keep in mind the needs of your family and don't commandeer space that might jeopardize family harmony.

Considering Your Background

Putting profit goals aside, if there is a single word to guide you as you select a home business, it's background. Build on your background. The skills you have developed and the contacts you have made while working your primary job or while pursuing special interests can be the foundation for your second occupation. By building on your past, you will have a running start.

Make a detailed inventory of your work experiences, from part-time summer jobs to professional full-time positions. Include your education, expertise, and training on the list because information and knowledge can be converted into a commodity with a price tag. Also include volunteer work and your interests and hobbies. Hobbyists usually have the equipment and talent necessary to get a business underway, and it's a matter of converting what they have been doing for pleasure into profit-making ventures. Use Figure 1.2 to help you define your fields of experience.

FIGURE 1.2: Build On Your Background

As you consider the type of work you might undertake, think about your background and how you might use your experiences to start a business.

List work experiences, hobbies, volunteer activities, and your special interests. Also take into account your personality and how you like to spend your time, along with your physical characteristics. Study the list and think about how to use your background and strengths to build a business.

Work experiences — listing most recent work first

_____

_____

_____

_____

Education — schools, degrees, special knowledge

_____

_____

_____

_____

Special skills you have developed

_____

_____

_____

_____

Hobbies you enjoy

_____

_____

_____

_____

FIGURE 1.2: Build On Your Background, continued

Volunteer work you have done

_____

_____

_____

_____

Special interests and things you've always wanted to do

_____

_____

_____

_____

Personality and physical traits that could influence choice of work (outgoing, quiet, empathetic, strong, frail, and so forth)

_____

_____

_____

_____

For years, I've watched a friend convert his interest in photography into a second income. Ray Billingsley was an administrator in the local school system. Through his contacts with students he was perfectly positioned to acquire contracts to do graduation photos. As years passed, many of the graduates asked him to do wedding pictures, then pictures of their children, followed by class reunions. The class and reunion photographs brought in extra profits because each photo contained the images of several hundred people and many of these people purchased a photograph or two. Ray not only enjoyed this venture and became the "official" photographer for many families, but he claims to have sent his four children to college on the income he brought in through moonlighting! When he retired from his primary occupation, Ray's photography business remained a vital part of his life, and it now serves to supplement his retirement benefits. So yes, plan to build on your background.

With that said, it should be added that doing what you know best may not be the most expedient route to business success. Just because you know how to do something doesn't mean you are destined to work at that occupation for the rest of your life, especially if the work will not yield a good profit. Too often, the advice to "Do something you know" sends people scampering to their home workshops to craft wooden ducks or knit or crochet doll clothes. But how many items need to be made and sold to bring in a reasonable amount of money? "Too many" is the answer, and many entrepreneurs doing this type of work have no idea that they are fated for failure because they haven't pushed around the numbers and figured what it will take to earn a good income.

Retraining for better opportunities might be in your best interest. It is the American way, and more enjoyable work with better profits may be as close as your neighborhood library or nearest community college.

Finding the Money

The amount of money you have to invest will certainly influence the type of business you start. Some businesses require a substantial investment to get underway while others can be started with little more than the cost of a classified ad in the local paper or printed handouts that can be placed on windshields.

Organizing group travel is a good example of a business that can be started on a wing and a prayer. A knowledge of the travel trade, some hard-nosed bargaining power and the ability to amass a following can yield healthy profits for travel agents.

For years, my husband and I have traveled with a couple who moonlights by putting together group trips. Dr. Donald Colton teaches music at the University of Evansville. He and his wife, Carolyn, invested very little money to get their business underway. They arrange and guide world travel during the many breaks in the academic calendar, and they have acquired an enthusiastic following by offering good trips at low prices. No place is too far or too exotic for them, and they are ever vigilant of world politics and changing currencies. My husband and I have traveled throughout the world with this couple — and 40 to 130 fellow travelers

— and we've happily paid the Coltons for their planning and expertise in making the trips outstanding experiences. Other agents plan domestic trips, taking groups to shows and sports events or on shopping sprees in distant or not-so-distant locations. But again, their success depends on developing a following — a group of people who regularly participate in the trips.

How much money can you invest in a business? Most part-time home businesses require very little start-up money, but if you must borrow money to get started, the rule of thumb is to have at least 50 percent of the needed funds before approaching a lender. Finding money to get a business underway is discussed in Part III, Chapter 6.

Evaluating Your Equipment and Location

Take inventory of the equipment and tools you own that can be used to start a business. Don't overlook the obvious. Your equipment might include ladders that can be used for paint jobs or a chain saw than can be used to clear woodland or cut firewood. A sewing machine can be used to make alterations or create clothing, and a computer can be used for an untold number of occupations (see Appendix). Do you own a van, truck, boat, snowplow, camera, lawn mower, air compressor, video camera, hand tools, musical instruments, garden tractor — what else?

The location of your home may influence your choice of business. Is there a lake on your property or do you live on a farm? Is a ballpark, entertainment center, or school nearby? Who passes your home and what do they need? Do you live in the heart of town or in a rural area? Are you near a highway, airport, or waterway? Each of these locations can be used as the basis of a business. For instance, many parents are uneasy about having latch-key kids, so someone living near a school might run an after school care center, keeping children safe and occupied until working parents can pick them up. Or, for those who live near an airport or highway, operating a bed and breakfast inn might be a good idea. This would be especially appealing to frequent travelers who might become regular customers. Someone living near a stadium could offer parking on a side lot or sell refreshments or specialty items (T-shirts, balloons) from their front lawn, and a farmer with extra rooms and a couple of horses might offer ranch hand weekends to the city bound. Try to think how the location of your home can be used to build a business. Use Figure 1.3 to help define your equipment, space, and location.

FIGURE 1.3: Equipment, Space, and Location of Home

Before selecting a business to undertake, it is wise to take into account the equipment you own, the amount and type of space that can be used for the business, and the location of your home.

	Check, if Applicable		**Check, if Applicable**
Equipment owned...		**Home is located ...**	
ladders	❑	near factory	❑
van	❑	near offices	❑
truck	❑	near school	❑
boat	❑	near stadium	❑
snow plow	❑	near entertainment center	❑
riding mower	❑	near airport	❑
mechanic's tools	❑	near highway	❑
rototiller	❑	in country	❑
sewing machine	❑	other	❑
kitchen	❑		
portrait camera	❑		
video	❑	**Space available...**	
air compressor	❑	extra bedroom	❑
baby bed, chair, etc.	❑	in basement	❑
computer, printer	❑	in corner of room	❑
copy machine	❑	in garage	❑
fax machine	❑	in barn	❑
answering machine	❑	on porch	❑
desk, chair	❑	in breakfast nook	❑
filing cabinet	❑	in family room	❑
gardening tools	❑	in workshop	❑

FIGURE 1.3: Equipment, Space, and Location of Home, continued

	Check, if Applicable		Check, if Applicable
Equipment owned...		**Space available...**	
excavating tools	❑	in kitchen	❑
vacuum sweeper	❑	other	
other			
		Grounds include ...	
		lake	❑
		horses, stables	❑
		wooded land	❑
		garden plot	❑
		space for parking	❑
		side lot	❑
		separate entrance	❑
		other	❑

Considering Your Preferences

As you ponder the various kinds of businesses you might operate, take into account your personality. Are you a "loner" or do you like being with people? Some businesses are people-oriented, requiring personal contact throughout the working hours, while others allow the proprietor to work alone at home. Even if you like to interact with people, you may get enough water-cooler camaraderie during the day and can forego this pleasure during your moonlighting shift. Do you like physical work or prefer mental activity? Are you creative or more inclined to follow less adventurous pursuits? Answers to these questions should certainly be factored into your plans as you consider business options.

RESOURCE: *Work with Passion: How to Do What You Love for a Living*, Nancy Anderson, 1995, New World Library.

What Kind of Work
Do You Have in Mind?

HOME BUSINESSES EASILY FALL INTO TWO categories. Essentially, they either offer a service or manufacture a product. But there are other possibilities. Some people build businesses around inventions, while others build on creative abilities such as writing, and producing art and crafts. Many use their own ideas to get businesses underway, but others rely on the ideas and expertise of others and opt for franchised businesses.

Offering a Service

The majority of home businesses offer some type of service, and many of them work nicely as secondary occupations because they adapt well to evenings or weekends.

Service occupations can be divided into several categories.

Business Services

With the number of small businesses burgeoning, the need for business services grows. Many small business owners subcontract work they either don't have the skills or the time to perform. For instance, some don't have basic bookkeeping and accounting skills so they hire outside help for these tasks. Large businesses also subcontract work. Barbara Stahura of Southern Indiana supplements her income by writing newsletters for area businesses to distribute to their employees; she writes other publications for distribution to their customers. Her clients have found it costs less to subcontract this type of service than to have it done by in-house personnel.

Business services include such diverse occupations as legal representation, equipment maintenance, marketing management, consultation, sales, delivery, typing, office design, secretarial duties, newsletter publishing, bookkeeping, and preparation of tax returns, to name a few.

Educational Services

From music lessons to advanced math instruction, parents seek diverse educational opportunities for their children. Many of these are offered by home workers. Also, adults who feel they need more education are turning to home tutoring, private lessons and classes to acquire new skills. Computer training is an especially attractive field for home workers as the emerging technology requires people to frequently retrain and upgrade their computer skills.

Health Care

One hundred years ago, most health care was provided in the home, but when the commercial sector created the health care "industry," illnesses often meant expensive stays in hospitals with unfamiliar surroundings and unfamiliar people. Today, there is a movement to again offer health care in the home as we look for ways to reduce costs and regain control over this part of our lives. Care is now offered by health professionals such as nurses and physical therapists who go into patient's homes to offer care. However, caring for the sick and infirm frequently does not require special training but depends more on vigilance, concern for the patient and the ability to follow directions.

Repair Services

Today there are all types of technological devices and equipment. When the equipment fails, we turn for help to the army of repair people, many of whom work from their homes. Not only do they repair sophisticated equipment, they also repair such diverse items as shoes, tools, office equipment, and small and large appliances — the list is continuously expanding.

Care Giving

Child care, and care for the infirm and elderly has become a booming business. Many home workers are providing this care, both in their own homes and in the homes of people needing care. Effective care givers need quick hands, patience, energy and a kind heart. While day care is a common business, few evening- or night-care facilities are available.

There is a need for late-hours care providers, making this a good opportunity for moonlighters.

Food Services

Food services range from preparing and serving catered meals for special events to baking pies for the corner restaurant or canning gourmet treats to sell at gift shops. While most caterers prepare foods for weddings and other large gatherings, one young man in my hometown prepares meals for busy families and offers a menu of complete meals. He doesn't do single meals; instead, he prepares ten meals at a time for two or more people. He does the shopping, prepares the food in his clients' homes, then places it in their freezers for later use. This service is reasonably priced and is attracting a clientele of people who are too busy to prepare home-cooked meals.

Home Services

The demand for home services is growing as the number of two-income families increases. People are earning extra income but lack the time to keep their homes clean and in repair. Many busy people rely on service businesses to help them. House cleaning and maintenance services have virtually mushroomed in the last few years, with many operating from home offices. Maintenance occupations include such services as painting, lawn care, and window, gutter, fireplace, carpet, and drapery cleaning, to name a few.

Personal Services

As business and social lives become more hectic, people are seeking help with their personal lives. Personal services include grocery and gift shopping, hair care and manicuring, financial advice, and party planning. Such mundane services as addressing seasonal cards and putting up Christmas trees and decorations are also being offered.

Manufacturing a Product

A wide variety of products can be manufactured in a home shop. While some manufacturing requires barn-like space, expensive equipment and is dirty and noisy, other kinds of manufacturing can be done in a spare room, garage, or basement with inexpensive equipment, and only the hum of unobtrusive machinery breaking the silence.

Finding a product to fabricate is the first consideration for someone interested in manufacturing. This can be done either by going directly to large manufacturers and asking if management is interested in sub-contracting a component. You can also use your own or another person's invention, idea, or pattern as a basis for manufacturing (see "Inventions" later in this chapter).

There are several places to look for product lines. Government-owned patents are available to the public on a nonexclusive, royalty-free basis, and private patents are also available for licensing or sale. Many of these products require a large initial tooling-up process, but it could be worth the initial cost if a ready market exists and the product offers the prospect of long-term return on your investment.

Information on private and government-owned patents may be obtained from the U.S. Patent Office, Department of Commerce, Washington, DC 20231. Inventors' shows are another good place to seek out possible products for manufacture. To learn when and where such events take place, write to the Office of Inventions and Innovations, National Bureau of Standards, Washington, DC 20234.

The next important issue to consider as you contemplate a manufac-turing business is outlets for your products. How and to whom will your wares be sold? There is the perception that most sales are to indi-viduals, but many of the biggest customers and best sales opportunities are to other businesses and the government. Large businesses some-times subcontract with smaller ones to produce components used in the manufacture of their products. This is known as "outsourcing." A small component may seem monetarily insignificant at first glance, but it can generate a lot of money when purchased in quantity. Even the large auto makers subcontract parts used in their cars; one subcon-tracts the knob ornament used at the end of shift sticks, another sub-contracts pads that cover the accelerator and brake pedals. This is a common practice that makes large and small businesses synergistic partners. The advantage of manufacturing a component for a larger manufacturer or the government is that once you acquire a contract, you will no longer need to spend time and money marketing your product. On the other hand, subcontractors are somewhat vulnerable in that their prosperity is dependent on the vicissitudes of the business with which they are connected.

You may prefer to manufacture a complete item instead of a component. Outlets for manufactured articles include the government, exporters, wholesalers, catalog houses, and retail shops; or, you can retail the items yourself. It takes time, money, and marketing savvy to develop markets for manufactured products. Marketing methods for doing this are discussed in Chapters 12 and 13.

RESOURCE: *How to Sell What You Make*, Paul Gerhards, 1996, Stackpole.

Inventing: A Moonlighter's Dream Business

Inventors and inventions play a role in many home businesses, but inventions require careful management to yield a profit. Most inventors have full-time jobs and putter around in their basements in the evenings just for fun. It is important to avoid conflict of interest issues when working as an inventor. Businesses sometimes require employees to sign an agreement stating that inventions conceived while working for them become the property of the business, but others don't object to employees inventing items in their spare time, and they don't claim ownership of the inventions.

Inventors have several options for earning money from their creations.

1. Sell the invention outright to a business that will manufacture it.

2. License the invention to a business that will oversee the production and selling of the product. The inventor receives a royalty for each item sold.

3. Arrange for the invention to be manufactured on contract. The inventor pays for the production and oversees the marketing process.

4. The inventor can both produce and sell the invention to consumers.

The first thing to do after creating the perfect widget is to protect it with a patent. Most home inventors think that acquiring a patent requires the services of a patent attorney, but patenting is a straightforward procedure. If you can invent it, you are capable of applying for a patent. Check your library for one of the many books that offer a step-by-step guide to the patenting process.

Few inventors get involved in the production and marketing of their creations. Most have learned that it takes a lot of effort to turn an invention into a profitable product. It also takes an astute business sense as well as money to bankroll the project. If you plan to build a business on a new idea or product, be sure to learn the necessary business skills or gather around you people who can bring your business plan to fruition.

If you invent a marketable product but aren't interested in manufacturing and/or distribution, you might consider either selling your invention to a manufacturer or licensing a manufacturer to produce and market it. Selling inventions brings a quicker income but if a company is willing to purchase your invention, that suggests the product has earning potential and you may make more money in the long run if you retain ownership and only license it. A license gives the manufacturer the right to produce products that have been patented, with the understanding that the inventor will receive a royalty for each item sold. The manufacturer is responsible for producing, marketing, and insuring the product.

As you search for a company to license your invention, keep in mind that finding the right company for your idea can be a time-consuming process. But persistence will usually yield success. Send your proposal only to manufacturers that produce similar products. The names and addresses of manufacturers can be found in the *Thomas Register*, a multi-volumed reference that lists manufacturers throughout the country. This reference is available in most well-appointed libraries.

The terms of agreement between the manufacturer and the inventor should be defined in a contract that includes when the product will be available to the public, the royalty schedule and the size of the first run. In order to keep the product before the public, the contract should include a provision that, if the manufacturer does not sell a given number of items within a specified time, the contract is null and void and the invention can be taken to another manufacturer. But remember, it takes time to get a new product on the market, so be lenient in giving the manufacturer time to produce and market an invention before considering another manufacturer.

Don't expect overnight success with an invention. It takes time — sometimes many years — to see an idea accepted by a manufacturer and for the inventor to finally receive royalties from sales.

RESOURCE: *Turning Your Great Idea into a Great Success*, Judy Ryder, 1995, Petersons Pacesetter.

How to Protect Your Idea-Invention for Under 30 Dollars, Terry Cupples, 1991, Why Didn't I Publisher.

Selling by Mail Order

Home businesses can become involved with mail order in several ways.

> Some function as distributors by purchasing merchandise from manufacturers or importers and selling it to customers who order by mail or phone.

> Home manufacturers and hand crafters sometimes sell their products to mail-order businesses or catalog houses who, in turn, sell the items to consumers.

> Others use mail order techniques to sell their own home-manufactured or crafted products directly to consumers.

For years, while writing monthly columns for several national business magazines, I received more mail from home workers interested in mail order sales than any other subject. These people had heard there is money to be made, and they were hoping to cash in on this lucrative business.

Success in mail order depends on offering a needed or attractive product or service, accurately targeting the market, effectively advertising and attracting customers, and carefully controlling the cost of doing business.

Mail order is an excellent business for moonlighters. Since a mail-order business does not require a store front or office in a business district, it can fit nicely into a home if there is room to store goods and process orders, along with an office to plot strategy and keep records. Mail-order businesses using the "drop ship" method don't even require storage space because these entrepreneurs don't handle the products they sell. Instead, orders received by the mail-order business are passed on to the distributors or manufacturers of the products, and the items are shipped directly to customers. Consequently, the mail-order entrepreneur has no inventory, little investment, and only pays the manufacturer or distributor for articles after they are ordered, paid for, and shipped.

You might consider operating from a postal box if a mail-order business interests you. This takes the activity out of your neighborhood, and neighbors will have no reason to challenge your business venture. Also, if your home is in a zone that does not permit businesses, but the post office is in a commercial zone, a postal box number is all that is needed to allow you to work without the special-use permit required by some communities. A street address is necessary if you receive goods via United Parcel Service (UPS) because UPS does not deliver to post office boxes. By the way, "mail order" should probably be called "phone order" because nowadays most mail-order sales are actually done by calling an 800 number rather than by mail. For this reason, you may need to hire an answering service to take orders when you are working your primary job.

Mail-order businesses range from those selling a single product to those selling a whole catalog of merchandise. Generally, the most profitable mail-order businesses are those that attract repeat customers. Customers will reorder from a company that offers good prices, good service and products that are consumed. Companies that sell gift items, vitamins, cosmetics or other consumables can expect repeat business because these items become depleted and need to be repurchased periodically. If customers are satisfied with the products and service they receive with their first order, they will likely order more goods if they continue to receive mailings from the mail-order company.

At the other extreme are mail-order businesses that sell only one product, and many of these expect to make only one sale to each customer. These companies survive without repeat business because a large profit margin provides enough money for more advertising.

The biggest issue confronting mail-order entrepreneurs, besides where to acquire merchandise, is how to advertise their goods. Advertising is the most expensive part of a mail-order operation, and the success of a mail-order business depends on the effectiveness of its advertising and promotional campaigns. A discussion of advertising and marketing techniques used by mail-order businesses is presented in Chapter 12.

If a mail-order business appeals to you, study the market carefully to find a product or service you might offer. Answer advertisements and study the catalogs, sales letters, brochures, and other literature you receive to learn why these companies survive in a competitive market.

Many excellent books explain how to start and operate mail-order businesses and how to sell to catalog houses.

RESOURCES: *Home-Based Catalog Marketing: A Success Guide for Entrepreneurs*, William Bond, 1994, Tab Books.

How to Make a Fortune in Your Own Drop-Ship Mail Order Business, Duane Shinn, 1990, Duane Shinn Publishing.

How to Start a Mail Order Business, Edward Allyn, 1987, Allyn Air.

How to Start and Operate a Mail Order Business, Julian Simon, 1987, McGraw-Hill.

Mail Order Moonlighting, Cecil Hoge, 1988, Ten Speed Press.

Mail Order Selling: How to Market Almost Anything by Mail, Irving Burstiner, 1989, Prentice Hall.

Mail Order Success Secrets, Tyler Hicks, 1990, Prima Publishing.

Sell Anything by Mail, Frank Jefkins, 1990, Bob Adams Inc.

Writing, Creating Art, and Handcrafting

Creative workers thrive at home where they have the freedom to try original ideas and the time to develop their skills.

Writing for Profit

Writing is one of the more enjoyable home businesses that can be pursued in one's spare time. The problem is, most people who try to earn extra income through writing don't understand how to go about getting their work published, and they don't know how to convert their writing skills into cash. It's important to understand the publishing world if your goal is to develop a writing business.

Publishers are entrepreneurs, and profit motivates the publishing world; that's the reality of the writing/publishing business. Publishers need manuscripts that can be converted into profit-earning publications. Many writers remain unpublished and unread because they are unwilling to focus on the needs of publishers, and they continue to write what they want, whether or not a publisher will print the manuscripts they produce.

Most writers work at home. Some spend their entire workday at keyboards knocking out articles, columns, or chapters for books. Others have found that working another job during the day enhances their writing careers. Plots and characters brew in the backs of their minds, and they can hardly wait to get home from their day jobs to rev up word processors and pick up story lines where they left them the evening before. Some of these part-timers earn more than respect through their efforts — they bring in a second income.

A friend of mine, Jerriann Rust, is a school teacher. She has been so successful at writing and selling true romance stories that she gave up her teaching job, intending to write full time. What she didn't realize was that her source of material had been the steamy stories she picked up in the teachers' lounge. Cut off from this rich resource, her writing suffered until she returned to teaching. This enabled her to resume her moonlighting writing career.

Perhaps you have thought about writing for profit and would like to give it a try. Writers have several options for earning money at home. You might look no further than your immediate area and seek work from businesses, political organizations, and civic groups preparing newsletters, instructional and organizational manuals, and writing promotional materials for brochures and advertisements. Or, you could freelance for your hometown newspaper. Businesses and political and civic groups normally pay relatively well, but newspapers have a well-earned reputation for paying very little for freelance material. Another option is to address the national market by either writing book manuscripts or crafting articles, short stories, or columns for magazines.

If you decide to write for the national market and intend to regularly sell your work, you should write the kind of material that is easiest to sell. Surveys have repeatedly shown that nine times more nonfiction is printed than fiction, so it is wise to concentrate on nonfiction. Still, it cannot be denied that there are those rare instances when an unknown writer of fiction "hits" and fame and fortune follow; only you can decide if you should take the gamble and go for the gold.

If your goal is to be in the business of writing and earn income by selling manuscripts, you must write material that will attract publishers. The most reliable source of income for writers is "how-to" books and articles. Poetry is difficult to get published and even if it does get into print, it rarely earns much in royalties.

It might be instructive to push a few numbers around so you understand what it takes to earn income through this business. The price paid for a magazine article varies based on the length and quality of the piece, and the circulation, quality, and price of the magazine in which it is published. The amount paid ranges from nothing (or maybe free copies of the magazine) to $1,500 for a full-length piece. Many magazines pay between $100 and $400 for a 1,000-word article. The beginning writer can expect the lower amount. A writer with more experience can regularly bring in $300 to $400 for an article. For the purpose of calculating income, let's figure you earn an average of $200 per article. To earn just $10,000 annually, you would need to write and sell 50 articles, or approximately one article each week of the year. An experienced writer can easily write 50 articles per year, but selling them can be a greater task.

Can you do any better writing books? It depends. On trade paperback books you can expect to earn a royalty of at least six percent of the list price of the first 10,000 copies sold; the royalty usually increases to seven and one-half percent thereafter. If a book sells for $10, you will earn $.60 per book. If 10,000 books are sold, you will earn $6,000. If 100,000 books are sold, you will earn approximately $73,500. Because of the increased royalty paid when larger numbers of books are sold. You need to sell a lot of books to make a significant amount of money.

I have discovered two surprisingly simple ways to increase profits for writers. Both involve shrewd marketing. It has been said that the best way to promote a book is to write another book, but I have found the most effective way to promote book sales is to write magazine articles that refer to the book. A magazine article can bring a book to the attention of many thousands of readers and, if a reader's interest is sparked by the article, there is a good chance that reader will look up the book and possibly purchase it. I've written promotional articles for each of the books I've had published and this has resulted in large book sales.

The first book I wrote described how to grow and cook mushrooms. It might have sold 15 copies if I were lucky! To publicize the book, I wrote and sold 23 different manuscripts about growing and cooking mushrooms. The articles were published in gardening, family, farming, and culinary magazines. Each article mentioned that I was the author of *Growing and Cooking Your Own Mushrooms* (GardenWay) and, as a result, the book sold beyond my publisher's wildest dreams and has gone through seven printings.

It's easier to get articles published in magazines after you have written a book because editors are looking for "authorities" to write for them. After you've written a book, it's assumed you're an authority, and editors proudly inform their readers that you are the author of such-and-such book. This plays right into your bank account. Not only will editors pay more for your work, but the publication of an article on the same subject as your book is essentially a free advertisement that dramatically increases book sales, which means you will pick up more royalties.

You can also keep a book before the public by becoming a columnist for newspapers or for a national periodical and write on the same subject as the book you are trying to promote. It is much easier to get a column after having had a book published, and this constant exposure will significantly increase book sales.

Authors can increase their share of the profit generated by a book by selling books directly to consumers. Publishers usually permit authors to buy copies of their books at wholesale prices, but they normally don't pay royalties on books sold to authors. Wholesale price runs around 60 percent of the retail price. If you buy books wholesale and sell them at the retail price, you can clear much more than if you receive only the royalty from each book. You would receive a $.60 royalty on a book that costs $10, but if you sell it yourself, you will make $4.

Giving talks to community organizations and at public libraries is a good way to build a public image and sell books. In fact, selling books is a snap. I have given over 200 talks on the subject of my last book and have enjoyed every minute of this venture. Not only have I enjoyed sharing the information and being covered in the press in the communities where I have talked, but each of these talks has resulted in book signings and sales. Once you start giving lectures, you will discover that innumerable organizations are looking for speakers and you will be asked to talk to many of these groups.

Increasing book sales sets a cycle in motion. When a book publisher sees that you can, and will, promote a book, you become valuable to the organization, and this makes finding a publisher for your next book much easier.

Even though the number of words published in this country is awesome, writing is undeniably a tough business. Good marketing skills are needed to be successful in the writing business. Thousands of publishers interested in purchasing freelance material are listed in writers' directories, along with a brief description of the type of manuscripts needed, addresses of editors, payment offered, and other information valuable to freelance writers. The most widely used directory is *Writer's Market*.

RESOURCE: *Writing: Getting into Print, A Business Guide for Writers*, Jo Frohbieter-Mueller, 1994, Glenbridge Publishing. This book guides writers through the marketing process and shows them how to find publishers for short stories, articles, and book manuscripts.

Art for Profit

Artists must be business wise and art smart to earn a profit: like writers, most artists work at home. Whether working with paint, steel, stained glass, clay, wood, or another medium, the home setting provides the security and serenity needed to produce works of art.

Like writers, artists must not only produce good work, they must also know how to market it if they expect to earn a reasonable profit. Most artists — even talented ones — have difficulty earning much profit through the sale of their works. If your goal is to create art and "hang" the profit, then you can paint or sculpt whatever you like. However, if your goal is to earn a profit from your work, you should take a hard look at the market, determine what type of art sells best, and concentrate your efforts in that direction. Artists who paint landmarks, churches, or well-known buildings can increase profits by having prints made of their work and selling them as well as the original paintings. Others attract business by painting pictures of the old homeplace for families, and still others lure customers by creating functional art such as stained glass windows or sculptured furniture.

I know an artist who attracts buyers simply because he's good at his craft. Tim Fitzgerald works with steel, and his unique sculptures frequently win awards. He creates commissioned pieces and regularly sells his work at art shows and fairs. While Tim has attracted a growing number of collectors, he fails to bring in enough profit to support his family. Art is Tim's first love, but feeding his family is his first responsibility. To do this, Tim works at a steel foundry during the day where he polishes his steel-working techniques and collects a paycheck. His boss knows Tim has talent and allows him to take home pieces of scrap metal that can be used in his artistic compositions. Tim is fortunate to have a good match between his occupations, with his primary job supporting and enhancing his work done when the moon shines.

As Tim and all successful artists know, the trick to selling art is keeping it before the buying public — in shows, malls, contests, fairs, restaurants — wherever people gather or pass. Techniques used to sell art are discussed in Chapters 12 and 13.

RESOURCE: *How to Survive and Prosper as an Artist*, Caroll Michels, 1992, H. Holt and Company.

Handcrafting

Handcrafting has become a huge cottage industry. Homes are literally littered with handcrafted items, and we can expect even more demand for handmade products as people attempt to soften the influence of mass-produced, machine-made items on their lives.

Most handcrafted articles are made by people working at home in their spare time. There's no place like home to stitch a quilt, sculpt, paint, or whittle. Some people are creating original, one-of-a-kind works, but the large majority use published patterns to fabricate multiple copies of an item.

Crafters can increase profits by using original patterns. You've probably been to craft shows where proprietors in several booths are selling nearly identical items. These people have used published patterns to produce their merchandise and are in competition with each other. Consequently, they are forced to reduce prices to attract customers. One way to avoid competition of this sort is to use your own patterns for your craft work. You can charge more for articles created from original patterns, and more outlets are open to crafters selling unusual items.

To earn a reasonable profit from handcrafting, locate suppliers who will sell you materials at wholesale prices. Identify possible suppliers by looking in craft supply catalogs, or look for names and addresses on the packaging of supplies at your local craft store. Importers and manufacturers rarely sell products to hobbyists but will usually sell to individuals operating home businesses.

Like manufactured products, crafted items can be sold either through wholesale outlets, retail shops, catalog companies, or exporters. Or, like works of art, they can be sold directly to consumers at craft fairs, exhibitions and the like. Each of these methods is explained in Chapters 12 and 13.

RESOURCE: *Start and Run a Profitable Craft Business*, William Hynes, 1993, Self-Counsel Press.

Starting a Franchise

A franchise is a relationship in which the franchiser provides, for a fee, a licensed privilege to the franchisee to do business. The franchiser offers an idea that can be used by the franchisee as a basis for their business. They also offer assistance in organizing, training, merchandising, and management. The number of franchised businesses is growing at a phenomenal rate. They now account for over $700 billion in annual sales, and franchising accounts for more than one-third of total U.S. retail sales.

A franchise business carries less risk than a business started from scratch. According to a study by Andersen and Co., 86 percent of all franchised businesses survive for at least five years compared to only 38 percent of non-franchised businesses.

Franchises have come home. For years franchises were directed almost entirely to entrepreneurs who operated from commercial buildings, but now many are being presented as enticing ventures for people who work from their homes and garages.

Magazines and newspapers are filled with glowing advertisements promising instant success with franchises. Protect yourself by being skeptical and informed because some franchises carry a greater risk than others. Some are offered by companies with a track record of financial success for the franchisee, but there are also high-risk franchises offered by new companies with an unproven record of success. The truth is, there are many franchisers who offer a viable product, method, or service, but others who are dishonest and anxious to make a fast buck from unsuspecting clients. Hence, you should be wary when considering a franchise, and if it sounds too good to be true, it probably is. One advertisement I recently saw went so far as to say, "Owning this type of company is a little like having a money tree." You should realize that no money tree has yet taken root, but lemon trees are out there waiting for the naive and unsuspecting. Still, even though risks are associated with this type of venture, buying a franchise is sometimes the best way to establish a business. Just make sure you are dealing with a reputable firm whose product or service complements your skills and goals.

Overextending yourself can become a problem when operating a franchise as a second occupation. A franchise not only requires an investment of money, but also a major commitment of time and energy. You must decide if you have the money, time, and energy to engage in this type of endeavor. Also, some franchisers may not be interested in doing business with a franchisee who can devote only a few hours each day to the business, but others will surely accept the money of all comers.

When buying into a franchise you should expect to rely on both the business skills of the franchiser as well as your own business aptitude and experiences. For that reason you need to evaluate your own potential for success as well as that of the franchise product or service. Compare several franchises that offer the same type of business. Magazines such as *Income Opportunities* and *Entrepreneur* devote at least one issue each year to the franchising phenomenon, and they also evaluate numerous franchises.

RESOURCES: The handbooks listed below briefly describe hundreds of franchises.

Franchise Opportunities Guide (A Comprehensive Listing of the World's Leading Franchises), 1991, International Franchise Association.

Franchise Opportunities: A Business Of Your Own, 1989, Sterling Publishing Co., Inc., lists nearly 1,000 franchises with descriptions and other valuable information.

The Rating Guide To Franchises, Dennis L. Foster, 1991, Facts on File.

Franchise Bible: A Comprehensive Guide, Erwin J. Kemp, 1990, Oasis Press. This book, written by an attorney, provides an explanation of the steps in buying a franchise or franchising a business concept.

Running a Successful Franchise, Kirk Shivell and Kent Banning, 1993, McGraw-Hill.

Telecommuting Opportunities

Telecommuting is a relatively new concept in the business world. It means employees work at home instead of in their employers' business space. What started with just a few businesses offering this option to their workers is quickly becoming a common practice, and starting in 1994, a week was recognized as "National Telecommuting Week." The practice has become so widespread that even Ford Motor Company, a business based on supplying transportation, employs workers who stay home and work rather than drive their Fords to the office.

The reason telecommuting is attractive to employers is because they have realized that when employees work at home, their businesses can be expanded and more workers can be hired without the cost of adding space and facilities to accommodate them.

Many telecommuters find that working at home allows them the flexibility needed to meet both work and home responsibilities, and several other benefits have emerged. Telecommuting is being touted as a way to mitigate traffic congestion and reduce energy consumption and air pollution. Also, telecommuters save on the cost of clothing, dry cleaning, restaurant lunches, and often they save the cost of child care because, as a result of the flexible work schedule, they work when their spouse is at home and can care for the children.

Telecommuting is a godsend for people trying to earn a second income at home because the flexibility of their primary occupation enables them to juggle it with their own home business, resulting in better use of time and more productive work. This flexibility enables them to operate home businesses that depend on daytime contacts, something that would be virtually impossible when working a regular daytime job. For most telecommuters, it doesn't matter when the work is done — just that it gets done.

You may be concerned that you will lose the fringe benefits provided by your primary job if you telecommute from home, but according to a survey undertaken by the Small Business Administration, there is no evidence of reduced benefits for telecommuters. The data, based on responses from 17,068 people, show both men and women who work at home receive benefits such as medical insurance, life insurance, and even paid sick days. Also, job stability was not affected by telecommuting.

Telecommuting occupations run the gamut of vocations from sales to computer-oriented jobs, repair work to manufacturing. The best way to find a telecommuting job is to look at your current occupation. If you like your work, discuss with your employer the possibility of working at home. To get started, you might work part-time at home until you establish that you can, in fact, get the job done, and slowly move more and more work home. Before turning in your time card and starting this arrangement, be sure to discuss how working at home will affect your employment status including benefits and promotions. You should also discuss if you can return to the office should the arrangement not work for you. You also need to understand whose equipment and supplies you will use, who is responsible for maintenance, and the many expenses associated with working from home.

RESOURCE: If you are unable to take your present job home, you might refer to the book, *The Work-At-Home Sourcebook: How to Find "At Home" Work That's Right for You*, Lynie Arden, 1994, Live Oak Publishers.

Now Is the Time
to Ask Questions

You have a specific business in mind. Before proceeding with business

plans, it is important to determine if the work you plan is legal and if it has

the potential to earn a reasonable profit. Defining goals will enable you to

make the business materialize.

C·H·A·P·T·E·R 3

....

Legal Issues
Concerning Home Businesses

THERE ARE SEVERAL LEGAL ISSUES YOU SHOULD consider before proceeding with your business plans.

Evaluating Zoning Laws

The purpose of zoning laws is to protect neighborhoods from industri-
al smoke, smell, noise, dust, and traffic. Zoning for home businesses has
its opponents and supporters, both claiming that allowing businesses in
neighborhoods will affect the value of their property. Those who support zoning for home businesses believe that to deny one the opportunity to work in their own home would reduce the value of their property, while those who oppose work in homes argue that businesses within
a residential neighborhood decrease the value of surrounding property.

Home businesses are illegal in some communities while others enthusi-
astically embrace them. It is wise to learn the zoning laws that pertain to
home businesses in your community.

Generally, small- to medium-sized cities tend to welcome home businesses, but they are discouraged and sometimes illegal in larger metro-
politan areas. Regardless of whether or not they are legal, residential
areas in most cities are bustling with home businesses. In the last few
years, a growing constituency has been pushing for a liberalization of the
work-at-home laws.

Citizens are asking that laws prohibiting home work be adjusted to
reflect the changing economic reality in America and to recognize the
advantages home businesses offer to both individual entrepreneurs
and the community. Some cities are changing the laws to allow home

businesses to function because they realize when people are working at home, they are not contributing to rush hour traffic and the stress on city facilities. A few communities have created areas with special zoning that encourage home businesses, and developers are building homes in these areas with extra office and business space to accommodate home workers. On the other hand, some planned communities or condominium associations have covenants or bylaws concerning the types of activities residents can pursue, and these bylaws can override a city's zoning regulations. Restrictive covenants are also included on property deeds, especially if the property is a part of an exclusive housing development. Check to see if your home is subject to these restrictions.

Most communities that permit home businesses usually place limitations and restrictions on the businesses to limit their impact on residential neighborhoods. A wise home-work zoning ordinance should be flexible enough to allow an owner to operate a small business but strict enough to protect the neighborhood from excessive traffic, noise, or the introduction of unsightly equipment into the area.

Some communities curtail the size of home businesses by controlling the amount of space in the home that can be used for business purposes, customarily limiting it to 25 percent of the total home space.

One of the biggest issues of contention is the number of employees allowed to work in a home. In some areas, one or two employees are permitted, while others have declared only family members who live in the home may work there. This ruling eliminates many potential home businesses.

Another issue that restricts home use is entry into the home for business purposes. Some zoning ordinances disallow the construction of a special entrance, limiting entrances to those already in existence at the time the business is started. With this restriction, space within the home sometimes cannot be used to the best advantage, especially if people visit the business, because entrepreneurs rarely allow clients to traipse through living quarters. Of course, getting around this restriction involves nothing more than having the foresight to first make the needed changes, and then start the business.

Extensive parking facilities are usually prohibited in residential zones. This rule not only limits the amount of traffic a business can bring into a neighborhood, but it also limits the kinds of businesses one might undertake at home.

A license is required in most communities to operate a home business, but in reality, few people bother to get one unless the zoning office contacts them. Sometimes a zoning office is alerted to a home business when a business name is painted on the mailbox or a "shingle" is planted in the front yard directing clients to the business. If the name of the business must be displayed to promote business or direct clients, it's worth paying the fees and chalking it up to the cost of doing business. Otherwise, there is no compelling reason to alert city officials as to what transpires behind closed doors. Still, it's worth learning the zoning restrictions and starting a business than can be brought into compliance should town hall become aware of your activities.

Organizing Your Business

There are several legal forms of organization for small businesses, including sole proprietorship, partnership, and S corporation. The most popular form for home businesses is the sole proprietorship.

Sole Proprietorship

A sole proprietorship is the simplest type of business organization, and it is subject to very few governmental regulations. This type of organization requires only simple bookkeeping and tax reporting.

The advantages of working as a sole proprietor include:

> Tax savings. You are taxed at the personal level, and the only extra federal tax form needed is Schedule C, which you file with your 1040. Business losses can be taken against income earned through your primary occupation, thus reducing your tax burden during the start-up phase.

> Few regulations. With a bare minimum of regulations, you simply set up shop and get to work. Closing the business is just as easy; file a final schedule C with your tax return and the business is closed.

There are several disadvantages to working as a sole proprietor. These include:

> Unlimited liability. Except for a few exempt belongings, your personal property can be in jeopardy in the event you are sued for damages or loss.

> No legal distinction between your personal property and your business. If your business fails, you are personally responsible for all debts, placing your home, car, savings accounts, children's college fund, stock portfolio, and more at risk.

Partnership

This type of organization is legally binding between two or more people. The two types of partnerships are "limited" and "general." A limited partnership is when an investor or investors fund the business but do not participate in the day-to-day operation. They are responsible only to the extent of their investment. A general partnership involves two or more people who form a business. General partners are personally liable for all business debts.

A partnership is usually formed when two people either like to work together, have complementary skills, or when two or more people need each other to finance the business and make it function. A partnership of two moonlighters could enhance the probability of success. For example, hours of operation could be extended if each partner worked different "shifts," meaning, of course, their primary occupations might also require different working hours. Or, if two people are needed to perform business tasks, a partnership might be advantageous. In any case, a partnership should be a complementary relationship.

One example of a successful partnership is the team of Steve Jobs and Steve Wozniak. Together these men brought us the Apple computer, and both were essential to its success. One was a master at marketing and the other was a brilliant inventor. A less sophisticated, but nonetheless good example of a successful and complementary partnership, is a couple of people working the craft market. One excels at creating and crafting items while the other takes the products to fairs and oversees the marketing aspect of the business. This same division of labor can be applied to a wide variety of businesses and may be a good reason to form a partnership.

The advantages of working as a partnership include:

> Few government regulations.

> Tax savings. Business losses can be deducted from other earnings to determine taxable income.

> Help in making the business function.

> Help in financing the business.

The disadvantages of a partnership include:

> Inability to make decisions without consulting the partner.

> Unlimited liability in the event of a lawsuit.

> No legal distinction between personal property of owners and the business. Thus, partners are personally responsible for all debts, should the business fail.

A written agreement should certainly be a part of a partnership. It should include how the business will be funded, how profits and losses will be divided, who makes decisions and what happens when one of the partners dies or becomes disabled. It is usually a good idea to use the services of a lawyer to facilitate the formation of a partnership.

S Corporation

The main reason businesses incorporate is to limit personal liability. A corporation's liability is limited to the assets of the corporation, consequently, personal property is not at risk if a business is sued. Most incorporated home businesses operate as S corporations, which is a special form of organization in which the IRS taxes the earnings at the personal level. Thus, for practical purposes, an S corporation functions much like a sole proprietorship, except personal property is protected. S corporations require officers and shareholders, and all of them must be U.S. citizens. The shareholders of home businesses are usually mom and pop, and a kid or two, and they also function as officers.

The advantages of functioning as an S corporation include:

> Freedom from personal financial liability.

> Ability to raise capital by selling stocks to investors.

> The enhanced credibility of business.

Disadvantages of forming an S corporation include:

> Cost of incorporation.

> Complicated procedures involved in starting and stopping the business.

- ❯ Recordkeeping requirements. Records must be filed on a regular basis with the state government.

- ❯ More complicated tax reporting.

- ❯ Stockholder meetings must be held regularly and proceedings must be recorded.

- ❯ Corporation tax levied in some states, whether the business is profitable or not.

If you are interested in incorporating your business, refer to the books listed below, or you may prefer to consult a lawyer to oversee the process of incorporation.

As you can see, each form of organization meets the needs of different types of businesses. Consider which form of organization will best serve you and the business you plan to undertake. Because your business will start as a moonlighting or part-time operation, you may want to start as a sole proprietor or partnership and change to an S corporation as your business evolves and your business needs change.

RESOURCE: *Incorporating a Small Business*, free from the Small Business Association, P.O. Box 15434, Fort Worth, TX, 76119.

How to Incorporate: A Handbook for Entrepreneurs and Professionals, Michael Diamond and Julie Williams, 1993, Wiley.

How to Start Your Own Subchapter S Corporation, Robert Cooke, 1995, Wiley.

Determine Business Potential Before Proceeding

STUDY THE MARKET AND YOUR COMPETITION to determine the probability of success before making too many business plans and spending money for space renovation, equipment, and supplies.

Finding a Market

It is wise to do a market analysis before starting a business. A market analysis should tell you if the business you are considering has the potential to succeed and earn a profit. Demographic information about potential customers will enable you to evaluate the customer base and determine if the demand or niche for the type of business you are considering is adequate to generate the amount of business needed to fulfill your business goals.

Strive to answer the following questions as you define your market and evaluate the customer base.

1. Do people need or want the product or service you plan to offer?

2. Who will purchase the product or service?

3. From what geographical area will you attract customers?

4. How many potential customers exist?

5. What are their age and income levels?

6. What motivates them to buy?

7. Is the number of potential customers enough to support your business?

8. Is the number of people who will use the service or product growing or shrinking?

9. Will people be willing to pay enough for the product or service to yield a reasonable profit?

10. Is the service or product being supplied by others?

As you prepare your market analysis, remember you can look for business beyond your immediate neighborhood. You can expect to attract customers throughout the city, in the suburbs and surrounding areas through advertising in the local media or by a listing in the Yellow Pages. You can also attract customers throughout the nation through a variety of advertising and marketing techniques (see Chapters 12 and 13).

Checking Out the Competition

Competition should be taken into account as you survey the market. It's not necessary to forego starting a business just because competition exists, but competitors will influence the amount of business you can generate and will probably cause you to spend more on advertising as you strive to acquire business.

To evaluate your competition, you need to know exactly who they are and what they offer. Your business growth and survival may depend upon knowing how to compete with the businesses already in place. Check the Yellow Pages of your telephone directory to learn who you will be competing against. Find out what competitors offer and the prices they charge. Ask for estimates. If you plan to do roofing, ask for estimates on your home. Or, if you intend to offer advertising consulting services, find out what your competitor would charge to do a variety of tasks. Keep an eye on the parking lots of your competitors. If business vehicles are parked in the lot, you might even jot down the names of businesses that frequent the place and call them after you get set up because businesses are always looking for better prices and better deals.

Compare your business plans with your competitor's business and realistically evaluate your chances of getting a share of the market. Take into account how much business is needed to make the effort worthwhile. Remember, your competitors are probably working full-time at their businesses and must earn their entire income through their occupation. You will not need to generate as much income because you will be earning part of your income elsewhere. You might also consider offering services that your competitors do not offer, or add a service. For instance, if your competitor repairs VCRs or lawn mowers, you might not only repair the same, but offer pick-up and delivery service. You will be surprised at how many customers will be attracted through this added service. There always seems to be opportunities for people with ideas and a willing spirit.

If, after studying the market, you conclude there is a need for the kind of business you are considering, and the chances for success are good, you are ready to proceed with caution.

RESOURCE: *Market Analysis: Assessing Your Business Opportunities*, Robert Stevens, 1993, Haworth Press.

Determine Goals
and Write a Business Plan

DEVELOPING SPECIFIC GOALS AND WRITING A business plan for reaching customers are essential to business success. The plan will enable you to proceed as though you were following a map to your destination.

Accomplishing Goals

It is essential to establish goals or objectives as you contemplate a business, and they must be firmly in mind as you begin the task of getting a business underway. Without goals you will have no sense of direction and no way to measure success.

Be realistic as you think about goals and expectations. Of course you would like to be rich and famous as a result of your work, but those may not be realistic goals based on the amount of time and energy you will be devoting to your business.

It takes more than a passing thought to develop worthwhile goals. Your goals need to be written down, studied, and edited until you are satisfied they truly reflect your objective.

Long-term as well as short-term goals are needed to get a project started and to keep it on course. Determine long-term goals first and then decide what short-term actions are needed to help you achieve those goals. Long-term goals are more general and encompassing but short-term goals are just as important because they serve as guide posts that indicate where you should be by the end of the day, week, month, or year.

While goals are important, remember they are little more than a framework on which to hang your hopes and direct your energies. Goals are something to get you started, but they are made to be changed. Build a "flexibility factor" into your goals, allowing them to evolve as you develop new ideas and as new opportunities arise.

Study the goals listed below and make your own list on the worksheet in Figure 5.1. Long-term goals might include:

> Developing a business that utilizes skills and talents.

> Showing a certain profit within a given time period.

> Integrating primary job with home business and home life.

> Enjoying fruits of labor.

> Teaching children about business and the rewards of hard work.

FIGURE 5.1: Goal Planner

Have goals in mind and on paper as you get your business underway. Goals will direct your energy to do the things necessary to make your business materialize in the direction you plan. Long-term goals are more general but short-term goals are needed to reach the long-term goals. Short-term goals can then be further divided into daily tasks which you should list on your daily schedule. While goals will direct you, remember they can be changed as opportunities change and you grow as a business person.

Long-Term Goals

_____

_____

_____

Short-Term Goals

_____

_____

_____

_____

_____

_____

_____

_____

_____

_____

Add extra sheets, as needed

Short-term goals are tasks that can be accomplished over a short time frame. They should be designed to help you realize long-term goals. If you are just getting your business underway, short-term goals include:

> Naming your business and developing a logo.

> Working out a budget and finding funding.

> Developing a work schedule.

> Preparing work space.

> Sending out news releases that call attention to your new business.

> Explaining business goals to your family.

> Identifying potential customers and preparing a marketing strategy.

As you can see, many of these goals are no more than the tasks you must perform to get your business functioning.

The wisdom of having written goals becomes very clear when nothing seems to be going right. This is the time to pull out your list of goals and ponder them. Reviewing goals will reinforce your resolve to succeed when you find yourself floundering and the work isn't going as smoothly as expected.

By the way, don't get so caught up in reaching goals that you fail to enjoy the process of reaching them. Some people work with such determination and a nose-to-the-grindstone attitude that the joy of "doing" eludes them, which reminds me of a verse by Witter Bynner,

> You must keep your goal in sight,
> Labor toward it day and night,
> Then at last arriving there
> You shall be too old (or too tired*) to care.
> (* added by author.)

Don't let that happen to you. It is important to include the goal of enjoying the process of operating your business or the whole adventure will be for naught.

Writing a Business Plan

Your probability of success will increase if you work from a well-conceived plan. A business plan doesn't need to be complex but it should ensure that business needs are met. The plan will serve as a blueprint for your business and guide you as you strive to reach your goals. People starting full-time businesses must make very detailed plans to guide their business management. This plan is not only needed as a guide, but it is essential for documentation when trying to acquire funding for the business. A moonlighting business usually doesn't require major funding, consequently the plan for a moonlighter doesn't need to be quite so extensive — it's simply a guide to help you find your way. A simple plan should contain the following elements:

1. A description of your service or product.

2. The method of manufacturing or acquiring goods and supplies.

3. A description of the competition.

4. A detailed explanation of your marketing strategy.

5. A projection of sales and target markets — based on market research.

6. A schedule of events and activities.

7. Funds needed, and if appropriate, applications for funding.

8. Your philosophy and approach to doing business, including the standards and values you will use as you pursue business success.

RESOURCE: *Small Business: An Entrepreneur's Plan*, Lee Eckert, 1993, Dryden Press.

How to Write a Business Plan, Mike McKeever, 1992, Nolo Press. This book explains in detail how to write and implement a business plan.

Involving the Family

Business people frequently need help, and many home businesses thrive on the help of family members. Are you expecting family members to participate in your business? If so, are they aware of your plans — and do they willingly agree to participate?

One of your goals may be to teach your children business skills and enable them to earn money. There are many tasks children can accomplish but it is important to keep each child's age and capabilities in mind as you assign jobs. As a child grows older, more responsibilities will help the child mature. However, in your quest to make your business grow you may be inclined to depend too much on your children's help. Keep in mind that children need play time, time to study, and time to develop creatively, and their work schedule should accommodate this diversity of activities.

A spouse can also be an important key to your business success if he or she is interested in becoming a partner. Because neither of you will have much free time, try to make the most of the time you work together to not only bring in extra income but also to strengthen your relationship. A spouse can also help by keeping the house operational and caring for the children. This type of help can be invaluable as you work at your secondary occupation, and it's important to acknowledge it as a contribution to your business success.

Subcontractors can provide extra help. Whether or not your family works with you, there may be times when you need some outside assistance. Rather than hiring workers and being burdened with trying to keep them busy during slow periods, keeping time cards, filing governmental forms, paying benefits, and the many other obligations that go along with having employees, it will probably be easier, less expensive, and less time consuming to hire subcontractors for work you don't have the time or skills to accomplish. Many subcontractors also work from their homes, and some of them are moonlighters. They can be hired to do specific jobs, whether it is your bookkeeping or creating brochures to advertise your business.

So, you've got goals, a business plan and help lined up. By this time you have already spent a lot of time and energy on business strategy but have little to show for your effort. What next? It's time to put your plans into action. As you start your business, keep in mind that making a business work and being responsible for its success is a wonderfully rewarding experience. Just be certain you are pursuing the right dream before your business gets so far along that it takes on a life of its own and you find yourself caught up in a project that will change your life forever.

Money Matters

Yes, money does matter. You must consider several monetary issues as you get underway. These include acquiring the money needed to get started, determining the appropriate prices for your work, establishing terms of sale, credit, and collection, and learning how to cope with irregular income. Each of these matters must be adequately addressed in order to establish a sound financial foundation.

Finding the Money to Get Started

IT'S BEEN SAID THAT LOVE MAKES THE WORLD go 'round, but clearly, it's money that makes a business go 'round. If you need funding to get a business started, this chapter will help you chart your financial plan of action.

Determining Financial Needs

How much money will you need to start your business and meet your personal commitments? Money from your principal occupation will probably cover expenses such as mortgage and car payments, tuition, food, clothing, entertainment, taxes, insurance, house maintenance, and so forth, but you may need a little extra for your home business, especially if you need to purchase supplies, office equipment, and conduct marketing campaigns.

Some part-time or secondary businesses can get underway with little capital and just a few customers. Since many secondary businesses are based on the skills and interests of their proprietors, the basic equipment and skills needed are usually already in hand, so it's a matter of expanding and attracting customers to convert a hobby into a business and doing for money what used to be done for fun. However, others start businesses from scratch and must purchase practically everything used in the business before they can get underway. If your primary occupation can provide for personal expenses as well as support your business as you get started, you are in the fortunate position of not needing to borrow money. Just be certain that you have enough money to carry you through the start-up phase and until the business starts to earn a profit. Use Figure 6.1 on pp. 54–55 to help you estimate your start-up costs.

FIGURE 6.1: Start-Up Costs

Starting your business adequately funded will increase the probability of success. Project the amount of money you will need, then seek the necessary funding. To determine the amount of funding required, list the expenses you anticipate including the cost of equipment, supplies, furniture, space renovation, advertising, and services. Each business will have specific needs so adjust the following list to your business plans.

Estimated Cost

Stationery _____

Other printed matter _____

Packaging _____

Shipping/mailing _____

Miscellaneous office supplies _____

Business specific supplies _____

_____

_____

Fax machine_____

Typewriter _____

Computer _____

Printer _____

Copy machine _____

Business specific equipment _____

_____

_____

Desk_____

Chair _____

Filing cabinet _____

Business specific furniture _____

_____

_____

Preparation of business space_____

Advertising for six months _____

FIGURE 6.1: Start-Up Costs, continued

Estimated Cost

Telephone service _____

Business specific services _____

_____

_____

_____

Amount of money needed
before starting your business $_____

If you do not have adequate funding to meet your personal and business needs, there are several places to look for loans.

Finding Funding Sources

Funding may be acquired from your own cookie jar, family and friends, private venture capitalists, financial institutions, or federal and state government programs. Figure 6.2 on pp. 56–57 helps explore some of the funding possibilities.

Your Own Cookie Jar

Don't expect other people to loan you money if you don't have some of your own to contribute to the project. Some people anticipate starting a business on somebody else's money but they quickly discover that isn't the way it works. You must show that you are committed to the success of your venture, not just through your enthusiasm, but by backing it with some of your money. In fact, you will need to provide a significant amount of the start-up capital before most commercial lenders will even consider contributing to the cause. Only after putting some of your own money on the line should you look elsewhere for additional money.

Family and Friends

"Twenty-five percent of new business start-up funds come from friends and family," says Arnold Sanow, host of the radio show "It's Your Business." Now is the time to call on that rich aunt, or any other family

---

FIGURE 6.2: Funding Possibilities

It is important to acquire enough money to get your business started and funded until it begins to earn a profit. There are many ways to acquire money to fund a business. Consider sources of funding.

How much money do you need to get started (see the Start-Up Costs Worksheet on pp. 54–55) $_____

Possible sources of funding:

How much can you contribute to your business?

                                                                              $_____

How much more do you need? $_____

Do you have relatives who might be interested in loaning money for your business? List those who might be interested:

_____

_____

_____

Do you have friends who might be willing to loan you money? Who?

_____

_____

_____

Private venture capitalists are looking for investments opportunities. Do you know any? Places to look (business organizations, networking groups):

_____

_____

_____

Financial institutions that might be receptive to a business loan proposal (ones with whom you have done business in the past):

_____

_____

_____

FIGURE 6.2: Funding Possibilities, continued

What kind of collateral can you offer (home, stock, land)? _____

_____

_____

_____

Federal and state governments sometimes make loans to small businesses. They usually charge a higher rate so they should be the last place to seek a loan.

---

member or friend, who might be interested in becoming involved in your business venture and contributing to your success. Make a list of the people who might loan you money. You certainly don't want to take advantage of these people, but they may agree to terms commercial lending organizations wouldn't consider. For instance, family and friends are sometimes willing to offer a subordinated loan, which means bank loans or other loans will be repaid before the family member or friend is repaid. Another possibility is friends or relatives contribute to the business through equity investments (buy a part of the business) without expecting any return for several years.

If you borrow money from family or friends, prepare a written agreement detailing the terms of the loan and how it will be repaid. Also, be aware that borrowing from family and friends could put a strain on your relationship, and this may not be something you are willing to risk. Special effort should be made to ensure your obligations to these people are met.

Private Investors

The most frequently overlooked source of funding for small business development is the private venture capitalist. According to Robert Gaston, author of *Finding Private Venture Capital for Your Firm* (Wiley), "Each year, more than 490,000 private venture capitalists, or business 'angels,' as they are sometimes called, commit $56 billion to new and expanding firms owned by 87,000 entrepreneurs. This represents 40 times the annual investment activity of traditional venture capital firms, and is the largest single source of external risk capital for businesses."

Gaston writes that most of these investors live nearby, are sensitive to the small business scene, and may be active in the chamber of commerce and other business organizations. They can be ferreted out by discussing your plans and networking at a variety of business and social gatherings. Private venture capitalists look like you and me, but they are always alert and watching for people with solid plans, the background to make them materialize, and the potential to make a profit. Call the National Venture Capital Association at 703-528-4370 for a list of members looking for projects.

RESOURCE: *How to Prepare and Present Venture Capital Funding Request*, Melvin Evans, 1995, Community People Press.

Banks and Credit Unions

Financial institutions rarely make start-up business loans, and they don't like to bother with very small loans. According to Howard Vondruska, administrator with the SBA, "It costs them about as much to lend $500 as it does to lend $500,000." Still, you may be able to interest a bank or credit union in your proposal if you: 1) have income from another job, 2) have gathered at least some of the money needed to get started from other sources, and 3) have solid or liquid assets such as real estate or stocks and bonds to use as collateral. When making a loan, financial institutions are looking for collateral, which is usually a house, other real estate, or stocks. They will normally loan 80 percent of the value of the collateral, less existing outstanding debt.

Insurance Companies

Insurance companies make loans to clients but this source is often overlooked. Generally, insurance companies use life insurance policies as collateral, and many use the 80 percent rule mentioned above, loaning up to 80 percent of a policy's cash value.

Government Loans

Both federal and state governments offer funding assistance to small businesses but they are more inclined to loan for a primary and full-time occupation rather than a secondary or part-time business. Still, if all else fails, you might seek a loan from the government.

FEDERAL ASSISTANCE: If your banker looks at your proposal and thinks it is good but is apprehensive about loaning you money, ask about the SBA guaranteed loan. This type of loan goes through your banker but the SBA co-signs, guaranteeing that the loan will be repaid. Your banker will apply for the loan on your behalf and handle the paperwork if your request has a good chance of being approved. Sometimes minorities, women, veterans, and disadvantaged people have more difficulty getting loans from private lenders. The SBA is sensitive to their needs and frequently extends loans to them. The rate of interest is slightly higher than that charged by a bank or a savings and loan institution because the risk is considered to be greater. Still, if you can't get a loan elsewhere, applying for an SBA loan is well worth considering.

STATE ASSISTANCE: An increasing number of states (and even some cities) have come to appreciate the role small businesses play in the economy and have begun to offer financial assistance to help them get started. Of course, most of this assistance is offered to people involved in full-time operations, but part-timers with realistic plans can also apply for this assistance. Call your local Small Business Development Center (SBDC) or chamber of commerce to learn what programs are available in your state, city, or county.

Applying for a Loan

A well-written and thorough business proposal is the primary document required for a business loan. Be prepared to give a professional presentation if you apply for a loan from a financial institution, private investor, or the government. You must convince the lender that you are a good risk. The proposal should be neat, carefully composed, and include: 1) a clear explanation of your product or service, 2) an overview of marketing plans and competition, 3) the exact amount of money needed, 4) how the money will be used, 5) a description of the collateral you will use to back up the loan, and 6) personal and business financial statements.

When presenting the proposal to the loan officer, dress properly, be well versed in your needs and the project you are about to undertake, look alert, and be enthusiastic.

Establishing Credit

Purchasing goods "on credit" will enable you to order merchandise, take delivery, and pay for materials within a prearranged time period. Purchasing on credit is a privilege granted to businesses that have established credit and have a good credit rating. Establishing a good credit rating is important because it allows goods to be purchased with money that is, essentially, loaned for 30 days. Those 30 days of credit are often needed to ease cash flow problems and promote business.

To "establish credit" means you have demonstrated that you pay bills on time and can be trusted to pay for the merchandise you order. This is also called a good credit rating. Credit ratings are assigned to businesses based on their record of paying bills.

When credit is extended, the normal procedure is to pay for the merchandise within 30 days after being billed. The billing date may be the first of the month following delivery of an order, or the billing date may be when the order is delivered. To encourage early payment, some companies offer a discount of one to two percent if bills are paid within 10 days of billing.

There are several ways to establish credit, but perhaps the easiest way is to build a credit history through the use of credit cards. As you get started you will probably need to rely on your personal credit history. For this reason, it is important to establish a personal credit record. Married women should open a checking account in their name only; incredibly, if the husband's name is added, the credit history automatically is assigned to his file in most cases.

Besides helping you build a credit rating, credit cards are convenient and can save you money by offering deferred billing. After your personal credit history is established, apply for a credit card in the name of your business and use it regularly to charge business expenses. This will not only allow you to build a credit history, but it will simplify bookkeeping and be useful when preparing your tax returns. The amount of credit you can obtain with a credit card will increase the more the card is used and as a record of prompt payment is established.

Credit card companies offer a variety of services, and it is important to shop around to find one that offers the services and benefits you desire. Many credit card companies do not charge an annual fee. Make sure the one you select does not charge interest if you pay the balance in full at each billing. You will also want a card that offers an automatic line of credit. This will allow you to make major purchases with the credit card, and you can then pay for them in installments. Since you may pay for some purchases in installments, it is wise to select a credit card that has a low annual percentage rate (APR). When goods are purchased in this manner, you are protected if the goods or services are inadequate because the credit card company will seek a refund or credit for you. However, some credit card companies charge an exorbitant rate on the unpaid balance, and it may be in your best interest to get a small loan from a bank to pay off the credit card balance. Banks usually loan money at lower rates than that charged by credit card agencies.

Some businesses issue credit cards to their customers, and some of these store-specific cards offer discounts, buying bonuses, and other membership benefits. You may want to apply for cards at the stores where you purchase a lot of merchandise, but before accepting a store credit card be sure to inquire about the annual fee and interest rates.

There is another way to convince businesses to sell to you on credit. Ask a few friends who own businesses if they will serve as credit references and vouch for your reliability. This is commonly done among business associates and is the quickest way to establish credit.

RESOURCE: *Loan Book: Complete Step by Step Guide to Getting a Personal or Business Loan*, Orlando Antonini and Casey Collay, 1990, El Dorado Press.

Small Business and Venture Capital, Rudolph Weissman, 1979, Ayer.

....

Pricing for Profit

DETERMINING THE PRICES TO CHARGE FOR SERVICES or products is a big issue for people just starting a business. The price you charge will determine whether or not you attract business and whether or not you make a profit. Many arbitrarily set prices without thinking through the costs associated with running a business and, more often than not, they discover the prices they charge do not generate the desired net income. Since this is such an important issue, the process of determining the amount to charge for your work is explained in some detail.

Building a Price Formula

A simple formula can be used to help you determine the prices to charge for your services or products. The formula should incorporate labor costs, indirect costs (overhead), materials and supplies, and the competition.

Labor Costs

Think about the type of work you will be doing and set a net income for one year that you think such work should command. It will be easier to figure what to charge for labor if you base your calculations on full-time work and make adjustments for your part-time schedule. If you will be doing work that requires extensive education, fine-tuned skills, expensive equipment or is dangerous, it is reasonable to charge more. Generally, professional and other highly educated or specialized workers earn more than members of the labor force who support them, therefore lawyers earn more than secretaries, architects earn more than the people who construct the buildings they design, and pilots earn more than the flight attendants and maintenance crew that keeps them in the air. Where does your labor fit into the pay scale?

62

Next, determine the number of hours you will work each year. This number should reflect the amount of time you can spend in the evening and on weekends in pursuit of your business. Also, you need to take into account the days you won't work. If you deduct two weeks for vacation, and two more weeks to cover holidays, sick, and personal days, you will work 48 weeks each year. How many hours will you work each week? If you work three hours each weekday evening and maybe 10 hours on the weekend, you will work 25 hours each week so your total working hours per year will be: 48 weeks x 25 hours each week, or nearly 1,200 hours each year. Full-time work would yield approximately 1,920 working hours (48 weeks x 5 days per week x 8 hours per day.) By working 1,200 hours, rather than 1,920, you will be working 62.5 percent of a full-time schedule (1,200 divided by 1,920.) Not all of this time will be billable. Some of it will be spent doing office work and the many other jobs associated with keeping your business functioning. Also, you will probably spend considerable time marketing your business as you get underway. At best, you can expect to bill 75 percent of your working hours. Seventy-five percent of 1,200 hours is 900 billable hours. Before calculating hourly labor rate, you must first consider the indirect costs, or overhead, associated with your business.

Indirect Costs or Overhead

Determine the overhead cost of operating your business for one year. This should include the cost of items such as office supplies, equipment, packing and shipping, advertising and marketing, business insurance, transportation, and home-use expenses. Home-use expenses consist of a percent (in proportion to the space used for business purposes) of the home mortgage or rent, home insurance, cleaning costs, interest on loans, maintenance, utilities, telephone expenses, and the like. The cost of converting home space for business use should also be included. Also include the cost of membership in business-related organizations, subscriptions for business or trade journals, and other miscellaneous expenses. Overhead costs will probably run 15 percent or more of your net income.

With these numbers established, you can now calculate the hourly rate to charge. The formula is as follows:

Target salary (62.5 percent of full-time yearly salary) + overhead expenses divided by the number of billable hours = hourly rate.

For example, if you plan a target salary of $50,000 but only work 62.5 percent of the time, the part-time target salary would be $50,000 x 62.5 percent = $31,250. Add overhead expenses (we'll use $5,000 as an example,) $31,250 + $5,000 = $36,250. Next divide by 900 billable hours to arrive at the amount you should charge per hour, which is $40.27. You may think that rate is excessive but have you noticed what you pay for services lately? Many home workers tend to underestimate the value of their time and end up working for a pittance. To ensure this doesn't happen to you, follow the formula to arrive at the rate to charge for your labor.

You must make two more calculations to determine the price to charge for a job. Multiply the hourly rate by the number of hours it takes to complete a job. If it takes three hours to complete a project, then $40.27 (cost per hour) x 3 (hours needed to complete job) = $120.81 — the cost of labor for the job.

Materials and Supplies

To complete the pricing process, you must add the cost of supplies that will be used to perform the job. The cost of materials that go into your product or the cost of supplies needed in a service business is determined by the price you pay in the marketplace. Calculate the cost of raw materials and supplies needed to make one item or to perform a service. Of course, you should make every effort to buy supplies at a reduced, or wholesale rate to keep your costs as low as possible. Add the cost of supplies and materials to the cost of labor to determine the amount to charge your customers.

Any change in the numbers plugged into the formula will change the price. For instance, if you intend to have a higher target salary, then the hourly rate will be higher, or if you reduce overhead expenses, then the hourly rate will be lower.

Competition

After calculating the amount to charge for labor and supplies, compare your prices with those of your competitors. Will you be charging more or less than the competition? If your prices are significantly above or below those of competitors, you may need to make adjustments; if your prices are too high, you will probably lose customers to competitors, but if they are too low, you may get the work but won't make a very large profit.

You might also consider a minimum charge for service calls. Let's say you repair garage doors, but when you arrive to fix one that is malfunctioning, you discover something is disconnected and it takes only a minute or two to reconnect it. Still, it is reasonable to have a minimum charge for such a call.

The method for determining prices for creative work is quite different than the method described above for other types of work. The prices one can charge for crafted items, art, written material, and musical performances rarely reflect the time needed to acquire the skills or the time spent actually crafting an item or presenting a performance. Frankly, it's a matter of charging what the market will bear — and it usually takes awhile to discover how your work fits into the scheme of things. If you craft articles to sell at art or craft fairs, the items must be priced competitively with similar articles being sold because shoppers will compare prices before making selections. The same is true wherever you sell your merchandise, so be aware of the merchandise or services against which you will compete.

As you can see, it requires both thoughtful calculations and a little common sense to determine the right prices to charge for your work.

Giving a Quote and Using a Contract

Some types of businesses develop prices through quotations, such as carpentry or plumbing. A customer inquires about the cost of having a service performed or a product made and asks for a price "quote" before deciding on who will be contracted for the business. A price quote is considered a firm agreement.

Take your time when determining your price for a job. Make the appropriate calculations based on the formulas given, and base your quotation on the calculations. Never just throw out a number because you could be stuck with a price that is way out of line. Figure 7.1 on p. 66 helps you work out all the factors to determine the price you need to charge.

While many people feel a handshake is all it takes to close a deal and they are comfortable working without a written agreement, others will insist

FIGURE 7.1: Pricing Planner

The price you charge for your service or product will determine whether you attract business and if you earn a profit. A price that is too low will attract customers but leave you with little profit, but a price that is too high will send potential customers to your competitors. The price you charge must take into account several factors, as illustrated below. After studying the pricing formula, use it to develop pricing for your business.

A pricing formula should incorporate labor costs, indirect costs or overhead, material and supplies, and competition.

Labor costs. How much income do you intend to derive from your work for one year? $ _____

How many hours will you work per year?   _____

Divide desired income by hours to be worked.   _____

Before determining what to charge for labor, you must calculate indirect costs or overhead. Overhead costs include the cost of office supplies, equipment, advertising and marketing, business insurance, transportation, home-use expenses — the cost of doing business. Calculate the cost for one year. $_____

Now, calculate the hourly rate to charge for your services. The formula is:

Target salary (percent of full-time salary) $_____

Add overhead expenses $_____

Divide by the number of billable hours   _____

This is the hourly rate you should charge for
your work. $_____

Next, determine how many hours it will take to complete a job and multiply that amount by the hourly rate to determine the cost of labor for a job.

Hourly rate $_____ x number of hours _____ = cost of labor to complete job: $_____.

Next, determine cost of supplies needed to complete a job and add this amount to the cost of labor.

Cost of labor $_____ + cost of supplies $_____ = amount you would charge to do a job $_____.

Competition should be factored in. If you are charging significantly more or less than competitors, you might adjust your charges accordingly.

on a written contract. A contract is a promise between two or more parties to do something. Most states recognize and enforce oral contracts, but the safest practice is to put all agreements in writing.

Write a contract to make certain there are no misunderstandings. Depending on the nature of the job, a contract could be quite general or very specific, identifying the work to be performed, who will purchase supplies, the quality of the supplies, when the work is to be completed, the amount of money the customer is obligated to pay for the service and when payment is due. The contract should be written in duplicate and signed by all parties obligated to fulfill it — which usually means the individual who will perform the work and the person who will pay for it. Each party should have a copy of the signed contract.

When setting prices, giving quotes, and writing contracts, always remember you are in business to make money.

RESOURCES: *Pricing for Profit*, Len Rogers, 1991, Blackwell Publishing.

How to Price Your Products and Service, Harvard Business Review Staff, 1991, Harvard Business.

Establishing Terms of Sale, Credit, and Collection

YOU MUST DECIDE THE TERMS OF SALE YOU will offer customers, keeping in mind the terms you offer could affect the amount of business you will attract. It is wise to become familiar with the advantages and disadvantages associated with various forms of payment and use the terms of sale best suited to your business. A well-conceived program of terms of sale, credit, and collection will help attract customers and avert a cash flow crisis.

Managing Cash and Check Sales

A "cash sale" is when money is exchanged for merchandise or a service. A cash sale offers the advantage of immediate payment and is the simplest, most desirable, and the most straightforward type of sale. Unfortunately, the days of selling for hard cash seem to be declining. For this reason, you need to be open to other forms of exchange and decide what terms of sale will best attract customers and allow you to collect the money owed to you.

Payment by check is also a way to receive immediate payment, although you will not have the cash in hand, and there is the chance that you could receive a bad check. Whether or not you should accept payment by check depends on how and what you are selling. It would be unwise to accept payment by check for a large sum if the customer is unknown to you, but smaller amounts might be acceptable. For instance, if you are selling items at an art and craft fair, it would be risky to accept a check from a stranger for a $1,000 painting, but it probably would be worth the gamble to accept a check for a $20 vase. Generally, it is safe to accept checks after comparing the appearance of the customer with the image portrayed on his or her driver's license.

Stimulating Business through Credit Sales

Credit has become the motivating force in the business world but it is only effective if it is managed well. Credit sales increase business. One goal of credit is to achieve the most sales with the fewest number of losses. As you develop a credit policy, keep in mind that Accounts Receivable is often the largest single asset on a firm's balance sheet. Also, in order to maintain good credit ratings with your suppliers, you need a credit policy that will ensure that your Accounts Receivable are, in fact, received, enabling you to pay your bills on time.

The primary cause of loss due to unpaid bills is a credit decision based on an inadequate credit investigation. There are several ways to evaluate the risks, and it is foolhardy to extend credit without first checking an applicant's credit history. The granting of credit must always be based on an applicant's ability to pay debts within a specified time period, but admittedly, it's difficult to determine with certainty whether or not a customer is a good credit risk. You can only base your judgment on a customer's past credit record, which is best revealed through credit ratings and credit checks.

Credit organizations can evaluate credit risks for you. Credit ratings are assigned to businesses and individuals based on their record of paying bills. A good rating suggests a business or individual can be trusted to pay on time. To obtain this information from credit organizations, you need to be a member and pay a yearly fee that covers a specified number of reports. An additional payment is required for each additional report. If your sales are local and you wish to use a credit organization, join one that investigates local businesses; a national credit organization is needed if your customers are dispersed throughout the country.

Some credit organizations do not charge a membership fee. Instead, a fee is assessed for individual reports. While each report may cost more than those issued by companies with membership fees, you may not use this type of service frequently enough to warrant joining a credit organization. Credit rating organizations can be found in the Yellow Pages under the listing "Credit Reporting Agencies" and include Dun and Bradstreet, and the National Association of Credit Management, among others.

There is another way to acquire credit information that could prove more economical for you. Instead of asking a credit agency about a customer's ability to pay, you can contact references supplied by the customer. Of course, you will only be given the names of companies whose personnel will recommend credit approval, so this should be taken into consideration as you evaluate the recommendations given by these references.

Offering Credit

Several kinds of credit are regularly used in the business world. Each is discussed below.

Open Account Credit

Open account credit means the customer can make a purchase and say, "Charge it" or, "Put this on my bill." This type of credit is usually limited to sales to businesses rather than to individuals. In order for customers to purchase on open account, they must first apply for and receive permission to have such an account. Open account credit is commonly extended to customers whose credit is trustworthy and who make a lot of purchases. Each purchase is recorded and at the end of each billing period — usually each month — the customer is sent a statement listing the purchases and the amount owed. Open account credit has some extra costs. It takes more bookkeeping and more printed material including statements, extra letterhead, and envelopes. It also requires postage to mail statements, the cost of collecting from delinquent customers, and the risk of overdue debts that may never be collected. Still, this kind of credit is commonly used among businesses.

Credit Card Sales

Of the various types of credit available, credit cards are clearly the credit of choice when dealing with individuals rather than businesses. The main advantage of offering credit card sales is that full collection of each sale, less the credit card company service fee, is assured — it's a matter of submitting credit card sales slips to the bank for payment. Also, you can expect more sales when you accept credit cards because surveys have shown that when cash is not required, people are inclined to purchase more items or services. Using this type of credit eliminates the need for a credit reference service, and you are never stuck with Accounts Receivable that are difficult to collect. The disadvantage of credit card sales is the credit card company deducts a small percent of each sale for its services, thus reducing your profit margin.

To learn how to offer credit card sales and the different programs available, look under "Credit Card" in your Yellow Pages, and call several of the banking institutions that offer this service. Some banks offer credit card services only to businesses that are stationary or those with walk-in customers, so if you plan to offer credit card sales at craft fairs or another type of business that involves traveling, you may need to search a little harder to find a banking institution that is willing to handle your account.

Credit card-issuing companies make money by charging card users an annual fee and a hefty interest rate on their unpaid balances at the end of each month. They also make money by charging merchants a collection service fee. This fee generally ranges from two to five percent of each credit sale, depending on the volume of credit card sales a business generates and the average dollar amount of the sales. The service fee is negotiable since there is so much competition among credit card companies. As you set up your credit card sales, shop around for the lowest service fee.

Is it better to allow customers open accounts, credit card charges, both, or neither? To answer this question you need to measure the costs of open account credit against the cost of credit-card credit. It pays to have open accounts available if the total cost of bookkeeping, printed material, postage, interest, collection costs, and bad debts is less than the fee paid to the credit card company. Also, you need to take into account that you may lose some business if you don't offer open account credit. But, credit card selling is preferable if your business does not have the sound financing needed to carry a large accounts receivable risk, if you don't want to bother with bookkeeping and administering a credit program, and if your clients do not insist on open accounts. Many small businesses use both types of credit, but the trend is toward credit-card credit for individuals, and open-account credit for businesses.

COD and Prepayment

When dealing with a new client, whether it is an individual or a business, the best approach is to be careful. Sometimes it's wise not to offer any credit. If you feel apprehensive about a client's credit rating, it might be wise to ship cash on delivery (COD). There is an extra charge for COD service, but most people realize this is the price of getting established with a business.

Prepayment is sometimes requested, and as the name implies, merchandise must be paid for before it is shipped. This eliminates the possibility that the merchandise will be refused if it is shipped COD. Like COD sales, this form of payment is usually used with new or unreliable customers. For service businesses such as a consulting service, partial payment or a retainer might be in order before any work takes place.

After several orders, you might offer the new client the terms extended to your trusted customers, but don't allow new customers to run up big debts until you are convinced they are reliable and will pay their bills on time. Of course, the system works the other way too. If your suppliers question your ability to pay, you may need to accept prepayment or COD terms until your credit is established.

Collecting the Money

Getting paid promptly for goods and services is a concern for most businesses and one of the hardest parts of working on your own. Mike Blout, a senior manager with Arthur Andersen in Tampa, Florida says, "Everyone loses some money. Everyone wishes he or she hadn't sold to the guy who had no money, or to the company that went belly up. With a few rules in place, you may take less of a beating." You should realize that everyone runs into a cash squeeze now and then and a customer might need a little extra time to pay a bill. Still, the following guidelines will increase your chance of receiving timely payment.

1. Be sure the terms of payment are understood at the time of sale.

2. Call clients with overdue payment. Find out what the problem is, and try to work out a payment schedule.

3. You might charge interest on overdue bills. This is permitted in some states but not in others.

4. When payment is not forthcoming, send a letter with a copy of the original invoice. Write "overdue" in red on the invoice and circle.

5. If payment is still not made after several attempts to collect overdue bills, hire a collection agency to represent you.

Averting a Cash Flow Crisis

Uneven income can plague sole proprietors in the first few years of business, and it continues throughout the life of some types of businesses. You may find yourself getting behind and unable to pay bills on time, but don't let overdue bills overwhelm you. Remember, birds have bills, too, and they keep on singing. One of the first things a beginning entrepreneur must learn is how to cope with uneven income and how to avert a cash flow crisis because a business can grind to a halt without the cash that's needed for day-to-day expenses.

Cash flow is the manner in which cash comes in from sales and goes out to pay for expenses. Controlling your cash flow is vital if you are to pay your bills when they come due, plan promotions, and cover unexpected expenses.

There are many reasons this problem develops, but the most common reason is customers owe you money but fail to pay promptly, while you need the money for more supplies and for operating expenses. It may be necessary to obtain a short-term loan to get through a cash shortage, although inspiring your customers to pay their debts is the more direct way to alleviate the problem.

If you appeal to a national customer base, the national economy could be a factor in your business, or if your business is regional, the economic conditions in the region could impact on your business.

Some businesses do better than others when the economy is stagnant. Those who do repair work know business is good during slow times because customers repair rather than replace products, while businesses based on generating new sales usually struggle during economic slumps. Of course, just the opposite is true when the economy is strong because there is a tendency to purchase new products and discard old and broken ones.

Moonlighters have a tremendous advantage over those who work full-time at their home businesses. During slow periods, you can continue to support yourself and your family through your primary occupation, and just hunker down with your home business and wait until the economy improves before going forward. On the other hand, being sensitive to economic fluctuations and to the public that responds to the fluctuations will help you take advantage of changing opportunities.

There are numerous ways to cope with uneven income and cover expenses. Here are some that would be appropriate to a small part-time business.

1. Make sure you have enough money before starting your business. Too many businesses are started with inadequate funding and, in their enthusiasm to get a business underway, many proprietors don't accurately figure the start-up expenses or the cost of supporting the business. This will probably not be a serious problem since you will be working another job while starting your moonlighting operation.

2. Find a few regular customers. Regular customers are like money in the bank. Working at home and meeting your financial obligations is much easier if you can develop a core of customers who regularly require your services or order your products.

3. Check the credit rating of new customers. It is counter-productive to make sales if those sales are to customers who can't or won't pay their bills. Check the credit rating of new customers before extending credit, and don't extend much credit until you are convinced the customers are reliable and will pay their bills promptly.

4. Invoice and send bills immediately after sales instead of at the end of each month, and send overdue notices regularly. The earlier a bill is sent, the better the chance of being paid promptly. If you are experiencing a cash flow crisis, you might offer a discount for quick payment. The discount most commonly offered is "net 30, less 2 percent in 10", which means payment is due in 30 days, but if you pay within 10 days, you can deduct two percent from the bill. This discount encourages early payment.

5. Bill in increments. On projects of long duration such as construction or remodeling, build incremental payments into the contract to protect your cash flow.

6. Plan ahead for expenses. There are ways to control the movement of cash. Make a chart showing when various bills are due each

month (loan payments, utilities, estimated taxes, and so forth). Wait to place orders so you will be billed the following month. Plan for the lean times by saving some of the income from busy periods. Also, don't plan expansions or take on extra projects, buy new equipment, or remodel until you see the momentum returning to your business.

7. Draw a minimal salary and keep purchases to a minimum. Fortunately, you can forego paying yourself in a time of crisis because you have another income from your primary occupation. There is a tendency to take more from a business when money is rolling in, but the best way to make sure you don't create a cash flow crisis is to take a regular, but minimal, salary until your business is well-established. If you take too much from the till, the financial health of your business can be jeopardized. Be patient. The time will come when you will be able to take a larger salary if the business is as good as you expect it to be.

8. Accept only work that yields a profit. Profit, not sales, is your goal. It is the profit on each product sold or service rendered, multiplied by the number of sales, that will determine your earnings, not the sales volume alone. Perhaps you've heard of the young lady who was ecstatic over the large amount of business she had generated through advertising and special sales. She still hadn't learned that it isn't the volume of business, but the profit on each sale that determines success. . . . and we heard her exclaim as she dropped out of sight, "We lose a nickel on every item we sell, but we make it up in volume!"

9. Consider leasing rather than buying equipment. When cash is tight, leasing may be the most expedient route because less cash is needed to lease rather than purchase equipment.

10. Take advantage of discounts for prompt payment when making your own purchases.

11. Review all costs for basic supplies and services, and keep looking for better prices.

12. Be flexible and go where the business is. Adjust your business to accommodate a developing customer base. As the economy changes, the needs of customers change, and it is in your best interest to adjust your business accordingly.

13. Spend less. While one way to avert a cash flow crisis is to keep money coming in, the other way is to reduce the amount of money flowing out. Work by the adage, "A penny saved is a penny earned."

By following these suggestions, you can expect a relatively even cash flow.

RESOURCE: *Credit and Collections for Your Small Business*, Cecil Bond, 1989, TAB Books.

P·A·R·T F·O·U·R

....

Getting Started

There are several preliminary issues to oversee as you launch your business.

First you must find a work space and acquire equipment. Next, you should

strive to create an image through a business logo, stationery, and possibly

a brochure stating your unique features. You will also need to develop a

bookkeeping system that will enable you to keep track of transactions and

evaluate your business progress.

Establishing Appropriate Work Space, Finding Equipment, and Supplies

THINK ABOUT THE KIND OF WORK ENVIRONMENT you will need for the type of work you will be doing. Some businesses, such as desktop publishing or number crunching, require isolation for concentration and uninterrupted work, but other jobs, like small engine repair, can be done surrounded by the din of family chatter and a lot of action.

As you search for work space, take family needs into consideration. The family was there first and it is unwise to take over someone else's space without consulting the affected individuals. You certainly don't want family members to feel they are being pushed aside to accommodate your business needs.

It is also judicious to design work space so it qualifies for the valuable tax breaks offered to home workers. As you set up your work space, keep in mind that the IRS requires that space used for business purposes be clearly defined and separated from living space. This important subject is discussed further in Chapter 14.

Determining Work Space Requirements

A typical office environment needs to be in a protected zone, separated from the rest of household happenings. Try to find a work place that has a door and a window. A door will not only keep traffic from your desk, but it will give you a sense of going to work when you open the door and enter the room and leaving work when you close the door behind you. A door will also protect your papers and equipment and will make claiming the space as a tax deduction much more straightforward by defining your space. A window will keep you in contact with the world, lift your spirits, and help you avoid the depression of working in an enclosed area.

If your house has a spare bedroom or den you're in business! If you're not fortunate enough to have the luxury of an extra room, look for corners of rooms or areas that can be screened off. You might find a nook in your garage, attic, or basement. Each of these locations is less than desirable but sometimes it's a matter of using what's available to get a business underway.

Try to avoid setting up shop on the dining room table or in a traffic area where you will be required to frequently move and shuffle papers and equipment. Too often, when a person "temporarily" works from the dining table, paper piles gradually grow deeper and deeper and the place becomes an eyesore in the home. It becomes too much of a chore to put everything away so family meals become less gracious and guests are rarely invited to dinner.

Think "efficient" as you set up shop. The focal point of your office should be a desk. A U- or L-shaped office arrangement will enable you to keep supplies, equipment, and resources within easy reach. As your work develops and you can see a pattern to your movements, rearrange the work area so you do not waste time or energy in unnecessary movements.

You can expect to spend a large amount of time in your work zone, so you might as well make it as pleasant as possible. I'm amazed at the austerity of most work places, whether they are at home or in corporate buildings. Strive to create a comfortable, pleasant setting, paying attention to the furnishings and the decorative items you place in it. You might include background music or even a peaceful aquarium to help calm your nerves and add serenity to your work space.

Deciding on Equipment

The Gallup Organization conducted a survey of 1,544 people who work at home and found the equipment used in home offices included the following items:

> Telephone: 98 percent

> Answering machine: 87 percent

> Computer: 74 percent

> Modem: 50 percent

> Cellular phone: 46 percent

> Fax machine: 40 percent

> Copy machine: 28 percent

> Pager: 26 percent

The typical office needs several basic pieces of equipment, and specialized equipment will be needed if you offer specialized services. Acquiring the equipment needed to run a business can be expensive but there are ways to get equipment and office furniture for little money. You might try:

> Going to garage sales

> Cruising the classified ads in your local paper

> Buying through discount catalogs

> Investigating no-frills warehouse stores

> Looking for store close-outs

> Attending estate sales

When possible, buy second-hand equipment in good condition, or consider leasing the more expensive items. In the long run, buying is almost always less expensive than leasing. The main advantage of leasing is less operating capital is tied up. Also, some leases allow you to change or upgrade equipment during the life of the lease. On the other hand, when you lease you are not building equity, thus, rather than building an asset through the purchase of equipment, your monthly payment is a liability. Whatever you do, make sure you understand exactly what is included in the price, have a contract, and make sure it contains in writing everything you verbally agreed upon.

Keep a detailed list of your home office equipment, furniture, and other valuable business assets. For each item, include the original purchase date, price, and serial number, and place the list in a safe deposit box or safe.

Telephone System

An efficient telephone system is critical to the success of most home-based businesses. It's via the telephone that you make contact with vendors, clients, and associates. Choosing a telephone can be bewildering because of the huge selection that is available, ranging from cordless, speaker, cellular, pocket, one-line, two-line and so forth.

You don't need to spend a fortune to acquire a system that is both efficient and cost-effective. Before adding an additional line or acquiring some of the many available features be sure of your needs. The two most important questions to ask yourself as you consider phone options are: 1) do you need a separate business line, and 2) how can calls be handled when you are away from your home office?

Do you need a separate business line? Before investing in an additional line, consider how many people use the home line and how often is it used for personal calls during the hours you will be open for business. The length of calls might be important, too, especially if there is a teenager in your household.

A business phone presents a professional image because it enables you to have your business name and number listed in the business section of the telephone directory and you can answer the phone with your business name. A business listing in the Yellow Pages usually more than pays for the cost of the extra line because it is targeted advertising. Surprisingly, only 20 percent of home businesses have a second phone line, according to Norwell, a marketing research and consulting firm for the electronics industry. You should probably install a second line if your phone is frequently in use for either personal or business reasons. Also, if you frequently use a fax machine, modem, or other peripheral, a second line is practically a necessity.

Should you have an 800 number? It may be worth investing in an 800 number if you receive orders by phone. Like computers and fax machines, toll-free service began as a novelty and has become a business necessity. Affordable 800 numbers are a powerful marketing tool and savvy work-at-home entrepreneurs are taking advantage of them. According to a survey conducted by AT&T:

> › Prospects who call are four times more likely to place orders than those responding by mail.

> › Using an 800 number as a response vehicle can increase orders by 18 to 23 percent, and dollar value per order by 20 to 40 percent.

⟩ Nearly one-half of all 800 calls are product inquiries, which reduces product returns by as much as 50 percent.

There is a modest installation fee for nationwide coverage and a monthly charge for this service.

Customized 800 numbers are also available, and these are valuable because they make numbers easy to remember. Kari Nash, of Evansville, Indiana, sold cremation urns via the two-step marketing method (see Chapter 12), and she used a customized 800 number that included the word "urns." This number was used in all advertisements and proved to be a valuable asset to her promotional campaign.

When the phone rings, answer it! There are several ways to assure that your telephone is answered when you are away from the office. An answering machine is the least expensive method, with many costing as little as $50. Several years ago answering machines were considered an unacceptable annoyance to a large number of people, but now their convenience is appreciated. The latest models include features that home-based entrepreneurs can put to good use. Feature options include indicating the day and time each message is received, alerting you to messages when you are away from the office either through a beeper-less remote or by an audible signal, and allowing access to recorded messages from another touch-tone phone by using a personal code. Some models not only enable you to hear the messages from a remote phone, but they also permit you to erase incoming messages after they have been reviewed, change your message, and leave personal messages to specific callers by using the personal memo feature. The remote features are especially valuable if you work away from the office much of the time.

Before buying an answering machine, compare the features available and determine which ones would be of value to you. Make sure the machine you purchase will allow callers to leave a reasonably long message. Some machines cut off after 30 seconds or so.

When using an answering machine, customize your message frequently so clients know exactly how to reach you. Be sure the message you leave is short and professional because busy people become annoyed if they must listen to a long pitch, so make it brief and to the point.

Besides answering calls when you are not available, answering machines can also be used to avoid interruptions or calls from friends. When you don't want to be interrupted, turn on the answering machine and hold messages until you're ready to return them, or use the machine to screen calls, answering the ones that require immediate attention but leaving the others to be returned at a more convenient time.

Call forwarding is another way to get calls answered. This inexpensive option allows you to program your phone to transfer calls to other locations where you might be or where someone else can answer calls for you. Calls are redirected to another phone by a simple dialing procedure.

If you are unable to answer the phone during working hours, but would like your calls to be answered by a person rather than a machine, then you might hire an answering service, and have your calls forwarded to the number of the answering service. The cost for this service is usually based on the number of connected minutes, with a base rate of around $30 per month, which would provide 30 connected minutes, or approximately 50 calls. This service can be located through the Yellow Pages of your telephone directory under "Telephone Answering Service."

Another feature you might consider incorporating into your system is caller ID. This service, which costs around $10 per month, enables you to identify each caller by name and phone number before answering the ring. An answering machine will only record messages from callers who choose to leave a message but there is no way to identify callers who do not leave a message. Caller ID records all who dial your number, whether or not they leave a message. I incorporated the caller ID device into my system because on many occasions I would return to the office to find 10 to 15 calls had come into my answering machine, but only one or two callers had left a message. Now, with caller ID, each person who dials my number is identified whether or not I am at home to answer the call. Since you will be away for long periods while working your primary job, this service could be invaluable to your home business and to the security of your home.

You might also consider a cellular phone if you are frequently on the road yet need to be available to your customers or clients. Cellular phones have become the backbone of many types of businesses that take people away from their offices. Many companies that offer cellular phone service provide the phone when the service is purchased. There is a monthly service charge based on the number of minutes on line. This technology allows you to take advantage of those moments when you are going from one place or job to another. Reception can vary and may not be adequate in your region, but if this type of service interests you, check it out.

Besides the other features you may purchase, your telephone should possess the following features if it is used frequently in your work:

> Automatic redial

> Mute button that allows you to block the sounds in your area from the party on the phone

> Speaker phone that allows for hands-free operation

> Memory for the storage of phone numbers

Computers

There are still some holdouts who refuse to get involved in the Computer Age, but the right computer with the appropriate software and peripherals is indispensable for efficiently conducting many types of businesses. Sure, you can do a lot of jobs by pushing numbers around by hand and by using an old fashioned typewriter but today, if you want to compete, you should be prepared with the proper tools. A computer is an essential tool if you are involved in the information economy or if you need to keep track of numerous customers and suppliers.

Computers are not only user friendly, but they are also buyer friendly, and while the number of features continues to increase, the cost of computers continues to plunge. Still, computers become obsolete so quickly, and for this reason there may be an advantage to leasing, rather than buying, a computer because it allows the business owner to keep up-to-date.

Determine how you will use your computer before selecting a system. This determination will allow you to select the proper software, and that in turn will direct you to the correct hardware. A financial consultant who handles financial portfolios would need totally different computer capabilities than an engineer who designs and draws mock ups, and an accountant needs still different features to track financial transactions. A writer needs little more than a word processor. It would be overkill to buy a computer with an excess of bells and whistles, although some writers transmit their work to publishers via a modem, so that should be taken into consideration. People who have a deep-seated fear of electronics and push buttons should probably look for the easy-to-use computers.

You may need some help to find the software and computer best suited for your business needs. You might turn to a friend who is steeped in computerese or seek the advice of the personnel at computer stores where both software and computers are sold.

SOFTWARE: Find software that will handle the type of work you anticipate. Do you need graphics capabilities? Will you use spreadsheets and need database software? How much information will you need to handle? Select a system that has well-organized and easy-to-use manuals because you and the manuals will become close friends as you learn to use the features your system offers. After selecting the appropriate software, you are ready to select a computer.

SELECTING A COMPUTER AND PERIPHERALS: Do you need a full- size computer with graphics or can you get by with a smaller laptop or notebook model? The laptop formerly had little power and was suited primarily for word processing and less demanding database work, but now, for around $1,000, a laptop can be purchased that is capable of complicated data manipulation and word processing. For around $1,500 you can get a laptop with a full range of features, including a floppy disk drive, hard drive, ample memory, and a full color display.

A laptop can be tucked under your arm and go with you to the terrace or along on trips, conferences, and other outings. A laptop is handy if you work as a field rep or as a salesperson, and it will enable you to turn your vacation digs into an office, allowing you to make notes, use a database, and access online data services. You can send and receive electronic mail wherever there is a plug-in phone line. Of course, a laptop can be used on a desk — it simply provides the option of being portable, and this empowerment allows you to carry your knowledge base around. By working while on vacation, you will be able to take that all-important tax deduction for business use for a portion of the vacation site, whether it is rented space or owned by you.

A desktop model must be permanently positioned but this type of computer is preferred if graphics and a lot of database and record-keeping work is to be done. The desktop model remains the most popular computer for office use.

Another feature to consider before making your selection is the technical support system available from the company supplier. Do they offer basic training, and if you run into problems, will the company provide assistance? When your work depends on a fully operational computer, it is necessary to keep working when your computer needs repair. Does the supplier offer a loaner while your computer is being repaired?

What computer system do your friends and other family members use? You will be surprised at the invaluable help you can get from friends or colleagues who use a system similar to yours. A quick phone call to a fellow user can answer a question that might take hours of studying a manual to answer, so yes, this is worth considering as you look at computers on the market.

Don't share your computer after you get it up and running. It's not that you're stingy, but if you allow people to introduce software into your system, it could become infected with a virus that could alter or completely destroy the files you rely on. Anti-virus software is absolutely essential if you share software.

As your business grows, so does the value of the information stored in your computer and on disks. To eliminate the risk of inadvertently losing this valuable information, regularly transfer information from the computer's hard drive to floppy disks and store the disks in a safe place away from dust, moisture, and extreme temperatures. Your business success could depend on the information on these back up disks.

COMPUTER PRINTER: When selecting a printer, the choice is between laser printers and lower-cost ink jets. Both produce black, smooth, letter quality printing. Laser printers are faster and can handle various grades of paper. They are much less prone to smearing or bleeding and the print quality is a little sharper than that of ink jets. Ink jets cost less and take up less desk or table space. Both are capable of printing regular pages, envelopes, and labels.

If most of your printing is word processing files, spreadsheets, and envelopes, you'll do fine with a lower-cost ink jet, but if you plan to print graphics, or if you know you'll be printing on various types of paper, a laser printer is probably your best bet.

One final word. While computer technology is a powerful tool, don't be misled. It takes both the right equipment and the right people to get a job done. A computer cannot replace skilled and knowledgeable people. And a computer will not make your business decisions. Still, a computer is a valuable piece of equipment that will enable you to produce correspondence and reports of consistent quality and format in much less time than when the work is done by hand or on a typewriter.

RESOURCE: *How to Use a Computer to Improve Your Business*, Ian Richards, 1990, Kluwer Publishing.

Computerizing a Small Business, Patrick O'Hara, 1993, Wiley.

Fax Machine

A facsimile machine, called a fax machine for short, is a highly efficient communications tool for transmitting documents through telephone lines — a process called "faxing." This is a quick method of sending printed material, instantly, anywhere in the world where there is another fax machine to receive it. No one needs to be present at the receiving end for the message to be transmitted, thus the process works during weekends, evenings, and holidays.

When the first affordable fax machines became available in 1987, they changed the whole home-office dynamics. Until then, home businesses catered mostly to local businesses, but the fax machine expanded home-business horizons. The fax machine is quickly becoming a staple in home offices. They are simple to operate and easy to understand.

Would a fax machine help your business? It depends on whether those with whom you do business also have machines. Some types of businesses use the fax extensively, while others don't use them at all. If you have a fax, but your customers and clients do not, a machine would be of no use to you.

The four most important features to look for when considering a fax machine for small-business professionals are:

> ❯ Automatic document feeder, which allows for the transmission of multi-page documents while you do something else.

> Copier function, the machine will double as a light-duty copy machine.

> Paper cutter to automatically cut each page from the paper roll.

> Auto dial and auto redial, a convenient feature that makes it easy to fax to the same number often. Essential if you fax to heavy-traffic machines.

The standard fax machine prints on thermal paper, which tends to fade and curl. Machines that use thermal paper cost less than those that use plain paper and can receive documents that measure longer than 11 inches. Most start around $150. If you plan to store fax documents for extended periods, you should probably look into a plain-paper machine, which cost a little more.

The quality of fax machines vary, with some capable of sending only written material, but others, with a higher resolution, can send photos, diagrams, and other graphics. You may plan to use a fax machine frequently and have a telephone line dedicated for its use. If not, be sure the machine you purchase has a built-in phone/fax switch. This permits you to use a single telephone line for both purposes. Some models have integrated phone and answering machine capabilities. Another factor to consider is the transmission speed, with the more expensive models faxing faster; fast transmission can save you money if you do much long-distance faxing. The size of the machines range from desktop styles to ones that fit into a brief case.

Modems

A modem is a device that will enable you to connect your computer, via telephone, to other computers equipped with modems for the purpose of interacting — transmitting and receiving messages and information. It is through the modem that you are able to access online services. The modem may be external and connected to the computer with a cable, or it may be internal. Another cable connects the modem to the telephone line. When purchasing a modem, ask about any terminal emulation software that comes with the modem.

With a modem in place, the only software you need to establish a conventional dial up connection to the Internet is a communication or "terminal emulator" program. This software will allow your computer to behave like a terminal, passing input to the remote system and displaying any output that comes from the remote computer.

If you have a modem, you may not need to purchase a fax because modems allow fax transmission via computer. However, some material you may want to transmit may not be computer generated, and that material will require a conventional fax machine.

RESOURCE: *Computer Based Fax Processing*, Maury Kauffman, 1997, Telecom Library.

Copy Machine

Making copies of documents is an integral part of nearly every business. If you need a copier, consider these suggestions. The copier you acquire should be able to handle letter-size and legal-size paper, and it should allow you to manually feed envelopes and odd-size paper. Calculate your approximate monthly usage and get one that has the proper "duty rating," which means the number of copies per month recommended by the manufacturer. This number can range from 500 to 10,000 copies. The more powerful machines are rugged and cost more, but it is unnecessary to purchase more power than you need. Copiers come in desktop models but the sturdier models stand alone. Be sure to understand your needs before purchasing or leasing a copier. Of course, copy machines are found in so many stores and shops now that it may be more cost-effective to pay per sheet and make copies when you are doing other errands.

Typewriters

Even though you will probably have a computer for doing most of the office work, it's handy to have a typewriter available for those odd jobs that take too much time to set up on a computer. Quick labels, maybe addressing envelopes, and filling in forms are easier with a typewriter. If you are purchasing a typewriter, get one with correction capabilities and a little memory; they are worth the extra expense.

File Cabinets

You will need a place to file papers whether your business is manicuring nails or designing advertising campaigns. Include at least one file cabinet in your work zone. This will enable you to organize records and maintain an orderly work area. File cabinets usually can be picked up for very little money through classified ads and at second-hand stores.

Desk and Chair

You need a desk with a large surface and ample drawers. Go for a larger, rather than a smaller surface so you will have ample room to lay out material and still have room to work.

The chair you select should be supportive, with rollers on a five-pointed star base. Be sure the chair is adjustable and will allow you to change positions during your work period to reduce fatigue. If you will be working long, uninterrupted periods, it is helpful to have a higher table where you can stand and work for awhile.

Locating and Buying Supplies

Finding the items to keep an office running will be as simple as visiting the office supply store in your city. Most stock a wide selection of office supplies as well as office equipment. A little comparison shopping will save a few bucks.

Locating supplies for your specific type of business can be more difficult and time consuming, so start looking for supplies well ahead of the time they will be needed. First try to find suppliers locally to eliminate transportation costs, and supplies stocked locally will be available on a moment's notice. Still, you probably won't find everything you need in your community and will probably need to look elsewhere.

To start your search, visit stores and shops that carry the kinds of things you need. Look on the boxes or shipping containers of the various items for names and addresses of manufacturers or importers. You can also locate suppliers by looking in trade magazines geared to the specific type of business you are entering. Advertisements in these publications should direct you to suppliers. The premier listing of suppliers and manufacturers is the *Thomas Register*, a multi-volumed reference work that is available in most well-appointed libraries.

Write the suppliers you locate, or call their 800 numbers for catalogs and prices. Remember, you must get supplies at wholesale prices or your business profit will be compromised. Until you find supplies at a good price, keep looking.

Locate at least two suppliers for each item you need. This will ensure that the delivery of supplies is not interrupted. Of course, you should purchase supplies at the lowest price possible, but should your regular supplier be unable to deliver, you can turn to the alternate supplier and avoid an interruption of your business. As you might suspect, being without a crucial item can bring your business to a standstill with back orders and unhappy customers.

A wise approach is to keep a large enough inventory to service your customers in a timely fashion, but don't turn your business space into a warehouse. If suppliers can deliver orders promptly, there is little need to warehouse stock. Inventory ties up money that might be better used for other purposes, so it is important not to be overstocked. However, during periods of high inflation, it might be a good idea to maintain a large inventory if the rise in prices exceeds the interest paid on the money tied up in inventory. But during a tight economy and low inflation, lean inventories can save money.

You will quickly discover that just a modest assortment of supplies can take up a lot of space. Keep the frequently used items within easy reach and store the remaining ones where they are readily available, yet out of the way.

RESOURCES: *The Complete Home Office*, Alvin Rosenbaum, 1995, Viking Studio Books.

Small Business, Big Savings, Laura Teller, 1994, HarperCollins, provides lots of tips on how to save when buying supplies and equipment.

Home Business Resource Guide, Cheryl Gorden, 1989, Blue Bird Publishing. Lists suppliers, training programs, and examples of home businesses.

Creating a Professional Image for Your Home Business

BUSINESSES LOCATED IN BUSINESS DISTRICTS look more professional than those operated out of homes but, with a little effort, a home business owner can create a professional image.

The most important part of creating a business image is attitude. With a businesslike attitude, you will convey to your clients that they have engaged the right person and come to the right place. Still, as this chapter will illustrate, there are many ways to improve your professional image.

Naming Your Business to Attract Customers

The name of your business should allude to the type of work that is done and, if possible, include your name. Examples might be Orth's Auto Repair, Kissel's Floral Designs, Moser's Squeaky Cleaning, or Accountant Services by Patberg. If your personality will play an important role in the business, you might include your first name, as well. Janet McCormick Marketing is a very successful home business operated by a woman who uses her personality to bring in business. She *is* her business, therefore it is important for her to use her name to promote her business.

After selecting a name, check the business section of the local phone directory to make sure the name you are considering is not being used by another business in your community.

A logo or a slogan aren't absolutely necessary, but they are a good way to create an image and reinforce the business name. A logo is visual and a slogan is a saying or phrase. Well-known examples of visual logos include

McDonald's golden arches, RCA's Nipper dog or Whirlpool's large swirl, and a well-known slogan is Maxwell House's, "Good to the last drop." Both elements can be used in developing your business identity.

Stationery and Other Printed Materials

Printed stationery is essential to convey the proper business image. Some people start their business without stationery and associated printed materials, but this suggests they have not made a commitment to the business. Stationery should be printed as soon as you name your business. The more you have printed, the less it costs per unit, but don't get too much printed. A 500 to 1,000 sheet run will probably be about right because you may change your business name, your address, or telephone number, and any change will make the printed material obsolete. You might consider using colored stationery to set your business apart from others. I have always used pink printed material so people know when they see a pink envelope or pink paper that it is probably a missile from me.

Besides stationery, you may need a variety of other printed goods such as invoice forms, purchase orders, and mailing address labels. Be sure to have business cards printed, and design your card to promote business. Business cards, often called calling cards, sometimes have only a business name, address, and telephone number. A much more effective card carries information about the service or product the business provides. While you might start with 500 sheets of stationery, a printing of 5,000 business cards is not unreasonable. Business cards are inexpensive, with a 1,000 or more of them costing less than $20.

You can probably use your computer to design the originals for your printed materials, using the various fonts and artwork available, but if you're unable to do this, a printer will provide this "set up" service for a fee. After paying this fee, the originals are your property. Keep all originals in your possession rather than leaving them on file with the printer. Printers like to keep originals because then you are committed to returning to them for future service, but that may not be in your best interest.

Using the Telephone

There is no way to tell, when talking to someone on the telephone, if he or she is associated with a giant corporation in midtown Manhattan or a tiny business squeezed into the corner of a bedroom. Be sure to take advantage of this fact. Proper telephone etiquette is good business, and for homeworkers it is also a good tactic.

On the telephone, you are your business and the way you present yourself directly affects your business. The two most important things you have to offer are service and politeness. Good telephone manners comes down to "Please," "Thank You," and "You're Welcome."

Keep a pencil, memo pad, and log book by your telephone. As soon as the phone rings, pick up both the receiver and a pencil and start making notes, even if you jot down nothing more than the caller's name.

When answering the phone, state the name of your business and ask, "May I help you?" Use the caller's name once or twice to personalize the conversation. Repeat important information to be sure you've heard correctly, especially if an address, order number, or credit card number is given.

Family members shouldn't answer the telephone during business hours unless they have been instructed how to handle business calls. A child answering your calls or dogs barking in the background can blow your cover, and it will become apparent to the person on the other end of the line that you are a small business working on the side. This is probably not the image you hope to project.

In order to create a professional business image on the telephone, use the following answering techniques:

› Answer business calls in an upbeat, professional manner, identifying yourself and your business.

› Never allow a child to answer business calls. If a single line is used for both business and personal calls, you or someone associated with your business should answer all calls during business hours.

› Be sensitive to the use of "call waiting," as this can insult the caller left hanging as you answer another message.

› Control the length of telephone conversations.

› Before making a call, jot down the subjects you intend to cover to make the most efficient use of line time.

> **)** Keep a record of long distance calls and check each phone bill for accuracy because billing errors are more common than you might expect.

Dressing for Work

Yes, you need to dress for work, but after you've put in eight hours at another job, the last thing you want to do is dress up for the evening or the weekend. Still, it's important to avoid the habit of slogging through your moonlighting job dressed in a house robe and slippers. The dress code in corporate offices has eased considerably in the last few years. You, too, can go casual, but you should dress for the type of work you will be doing. If you work in an office, casual wear is fine; if you are a baker, an apron and baker's hat are appropriate; an advertising consultant might convey the appropriate image if dressed in more dramatic "power" clothing. It is especially important to fit the job description if clients will see you. But remember, of all the things you wear, your expression and demeanor are the most important.

Meeting Clients at Home

A sign should direct clients to your place of business. If possible, have a separate entrance but, if this is not available, meet clients at the door and lead them directly to your office or shop. It's wise to keep doors leading to other rooms closed, and don't let clients linger in the family-used part of your home. While a pot of simmering vegetable soup might have an enticing aroma, strive to eliminate cooking odors during working hours.

Make your office look like you are all business. You would probably place pictures of your kids and spouse on your desk if you worked in a commercial building but it's not a good idea to display family pictures in your home office. Instead, hang business-related documents on the wall. These can be diplomas or membership certificates of trade organizations or the local chamber of commerce, or any other special documentation that confirms your business qualifications. Also, if an article about your business has been published, let your clients know about it by displaying it in your office.

Try to include something that makes your office unique. I have original stained glass panels hanging throughout my office and they always attract attention. A friend of mine, a lawyer, frequently meets clients in his home office where they encounter a parrot who has listened in on too many lawyer-client meetings. As a client enters the room, the parrot screeches "Alimony, divorce, alimony, divorce" ... and he continues this cacophony until threatened with extinction. This unusual tactic seems to work for my lawyer friend because it eases the tension new clients often feel.

You might want to offer refreshments to clients who will be in your office for an extended time. A small, dorm-size refrigerator is a good way to keep cold drinks nearby, and a tray with a few mugs and a pot of coffee will allow you to offer coffee. Don't disrupt a business meeting to run to the kitchen for this type of refreshment because this reinforces the message that you are working at home.

If you work amongst kids and clutter, designate certain days of the week for meeting with clients. During these days the place must be in order and the kids should be out of sight. Hire child care or do whatever it takes to make sure that you and your office or shop look professional and able to handle your clients' business.

It's important to have adequate parking space available even if it means taking out some lawn and laying down black top. A sign should direct visitors to the parking area. But again, the legality of this will be determined by local ordinances that address home businesses in residential areas.

Figure 10.1 on p. 98 is a checklist of all the elements involved in starting a business. It may help you see areas where you need to concentrate in order to get your business off the ground.

RESOURCE: *Naming Your Business and Its Products and Services: How to Create Effective Trade Names, Trademarks and Service Marks to Attract Customers, Protect Your Good Will and Reputation and Stay Out of Court,* Phillip Williams, 1991, Small Business Bookshelf Service.

FIGURE 10.1: A Check List of Things to Do as You Start Your Business

Following are some tasks you will need to do as you strive to get your business underway. Your specific business will probably require additional, distinctive work to be done. Don't start your business prematurely, before these basic chores have been completed.

- ❏ Decide on type of business
- ❏ Determine if enough potential business exists
- ❏ Check competitors
- ❏ Check ordinances affecting businesses in your community
- ❏ Develop goals
- ❏ Talk to your family about your goals and what you will be doing
- ❏ Acquire skills to do the work
- ❏ Determine funding needed
- ❏ Apply for loan, if needed
- ❏ Name business
- ❏ Check that name is not being used by another area business
- ❏ Design logo, if desired
- ❏ Prepare office, workshop, or business space
- ❏ Get stationery and other paper goods printed
- ❏ Find suppliers and supplies for business
- ❏ Acquire equipment needed to do job
- ❏ Make sure your homeowner's insurance covers the business space
- ❏ Get liability insurance
- ❏ Set up a bookkeeping system
- ❏ Develop an advertising campaign

....

Simple Bookkeeping Procedures

ACCURATE AND CURRENT BUSINESS RECORDS ARE essential for the effective operation of your business. They will be used to evaluate your business success, make business decisions, track accounts receivable, and apply for loans. Poor records lead to poor financial management, which is a major contributor to many business failures. Good records are needed for good money management, and while good money management won't make a business grow, it will allow it to grow. Bookkeeping is also necessary to prepare and document tax returns.

Bookkeeping is a method of systematically recording business transactions. Some home business owners still operate with "in" and "out" baskets, but that isn't recommended. Most home-business financial records can be adequately maintained by someone who has had no experience with bookkeeping other than maintaining a record of personal expenses, although understanding the meaning of debits and credits is practically essential. If these concepts baffle you, pick up a simple text that explains basic accounting theory and terminology.

There are many types of prepackaged record-keeping systems available, some of which are designed for computer use. Both the computer driven and manual programs lead you through the process of keeping records. For instance, SWIFT Home Office Accountant is an inexpensive accounting software package that makes it easy for the person with virtually no accounting experience and little computer background to keep books. It has easy-to-follow on screen directions that guide the user through each operation. This program will automatically separate personal finances from business finances. There are many such programs on the market, and they are available at computer or office supply stores.

Any bookkeeping system worth using will keep the most valuable information at your fingertips and allow you to immediately know: 1) cash on hand, 2) what is owed to you, and 3) what you owe to others. This information will be needed for the day-to-day operation of your business.

Records kept for the management of your business will be adequate to document tax returns. The IRS's only requirement is that you maintain permanent books that can be used to identify your income, expenses, and deductions.

Select a system you understand, one that is easy to use, and will help you see how your business is performing. The system you select should include a record of checkbook transactions, cash receipts, accounts receivable, accounts payable, a sales journal, and a petty cash fund. Each of these is described below.

> › Checkbook. List each check written, to whom it is disbursed, the amount of the check, and a notation explaining the purpose of the payment. This is probably no different than what you record for your personal check payments. Depending on the type of business you undertake, you may be able to operate with a single checking account. If a single account is used, each transaction must be clearly identified by inserting a code (maybe HB for Home Business) before each check or deposit that is business related. This code will allow you to quickly separate business from personal transactions.

> › Cash receipts. Record the amount of money received, the date of receipt, from whom it was received and the reason for the payment.

> › Accounts receivable. A record of the money owed to you, who owes it, the date it is due, and why it is owed.

> › Accounts payable. A record of money you owe, the amount of each bill, the date it is due, and to whom and for what it is owed.

> › Sales journal. This describes each sale and should include the date of the sale, customer's name, amount of the sale, and the sales tax, if any.

> › Petty cash. A container with money to pay for small incidentals needed during the course of doing business. Actually, you may just list the various items, pay for them out of your pocket, and

reimburse yourself from the business account when a reasonable disbursement has accumulated.

Plan to set aside some bookkeeping time every couple of days. The following schedule and checklist will enable you to keep records up-to-date and gauge the pulse of your business.

Each week:

> Determine cash on hand.

> Summarize sales and cash receipts.

> Record monies paid out.

> Send notices for past due accounts receivables.

> Pay accounts payable as they come due (or earlier if there is a discount advantage).

Each month:

> Reconcile bank statement. Check that the bank statement listing checks deposited and written agrees with your checkbook.

Each quarter:

> Prepare an income statement. This is also called a profit and loss statement, and it shows how a business performed over a given period. It shows the total income from sales and the cost of producing the product or rendering the service. Expenses are deducted from the gross profit to show the net profit or loss.

> Prepare a balance sheet. A balance sheet provides a picture of the financial health of a business at a given date. It lists the assets (what the business owns and accounts receivables) and liabilities (what the business owes). Net worth is the difference between assets and liabilities.

> Check that receipts for miscellaneous expenditures equal the amount of money removed from the petty cash fund. Tally the receipts and reimburse the petty cash fund.

> Check that tax payments are up-to-date. If you collect sales tax you will probably need to forward this money to your state revenue department every three months. Also, when you begin showing a significant profit, you will be required to make quarterly estimated

income tax payments to the state and federal government (see Chapter 14).

> ❭ Study inventory. Make adjustments to keep it at optimum levels.

It's a good idea to do your own bookkeeping even if you know very little about the process. By forcing yourself to review your business transactions in the course of "doing the books," you will be much more aware of how the business is progressing and more sensitive to what is succeeding and bringing in sales and generating profit, and what is not especially helpful to the business. With this ongoing evaluation, you will have the information needed to make positive changes that will increase sales and profit.

Although it is wise to do your own bookkeeping, especially as your business gets underway, you might consider hiring an accountant to prepare tax returns because he or she will know deductions and loop holes that escape those not versed in tax law.

While keeping books, always keep in mind the documentation needed as you prepare tax returns. This documentation is not needed unless you are audited, but don't take deductions unless you have the receipts or check stubs in hand to verify the deductions. Besides major purchases, you will probably purchase many small items out of pocket and it is necessary to save all receipts to document these numerous expenses. As the year progresses, the pile of receipts can become quite large, and it might be a good idea to organize them as you go along. This can be done by keeping each quarter's receipts in a large manila envelope, or you can set up an expandable file in which you place receipts throughout the year. Thus, you would probably have a section for postal expenses, office supplies, and the like. At the end of the year, make a list of various expenses according to expense groups. For instance, don't record each purchase of postage stamps; instead, group all stamp purchases together as a single expense, and so forth.

Keep all receipts and canceled checks in a safe place for seven years. These records are essential as you or an accountant prepare tax returns and should you be targeted for an audit by the IRS.

RESOURCE: *Bookkeeping On Your Home-Based PC*, Lisa Stern, 1993, TAB Books.

Bookkeeping for a Small Business, Diane Bellavance, 1994, DBA Books.

Getting and
Keeping Customers

Attracting customers is perhaps the most important part of operating your business. Whether selling services or products, you should be aware of the many different marketing procedures and learn to use the most cost-effective techniques. Marketing is an ongoing process, and the cost of promoting your business should be built into your operating budget.

Generating Sales through Advertising and Publicity

YOU WILL CREATE DEMAND FOR YOUR GOODS or services and increase sales if you promote your business through publicity and advertisements. Publicity is exposure that can be generated without cost, and advertisements are the paid part of a promotional campaign. Your goal should be to develop a promotional campaign that will attract customers in the most cost-effective manner.

Identifying Your Target Market

The type of campaign you undertake should be based on the people you are trying to reach. If your business is directed to people who live nearby — in your home town or your neighborhood — the campaign will be conducted quite differently than if you are trying to reach people who are distributed over a larger area, perhaps throughout the nation.

The majority of home operations are built on business that can be generated in the immediate area. This is especially true of the service-oriented businesses such as bill collection, wallpaper hanging, accounting, real estate sales, or party planning. Obviously, promotions for these businesses should be directed to the immediate area. On the other hand, a mail-order business or a desktop publisher would seek a widely dispersed clientele, and their campaigns must be designed to attract the attention of this scattered market. Techniques for reaching these two groups are described in this chapter.

Identify potential customers before embarking on a promotional campaign. Ask yourself the following questions as you seek to identify potential customers.

- › What are the defining characteristics of my ideal customer — age, sex, special interests, or circumstances (income, physical abilities, interest in travel or books — this sort of thing)?

- › Where do they live — nearby, or are they widely scattered?

- › What do they want or need — what are they seeking?

- › How can I meet their wants or needs?

- › When will they need my service or product?

- › How can I attract their interest?

- › What type of advertising would be seen or heard by these people?

- › How can I gain their business?

Promoting Your Business Locally

Promoting a business within a limited area can be just as challenging as promoting one nationwide, and a variety of techniques can be used to create customer interest.

Signs

One of the most cost-effective ways to attract attention and promote a home business is through the use of signs. This advertising tool tells people who and where you are, what you are selling, promoting your business around the clock, giving you high visibility at low cost.

A sign in your front yard or one hanging from your mailbox is not only a good way to advertise, but if clients come to your home, such a sign is necessary to reassure them that they are at the right place.

The size of yard signs is limited by the rules of zoning boards, but a 2 x 2 foot sign is commonly acceptable in residential zones. Some cities prohibit yard signs but will allow a sign on a porch or in a window, while others prohibit all signs on residential property. If a sign is not permitted in your neighborhood, place larger than normal street numbers on your house in a clearly visible place.

Inexpensive, painted wooden signs are appropriate in residential neighborhoods but neon, plastic, and electronic signs are usually prohibited; they are inappropriate even if they are legal.

When a business sign is placed in a yard or on a mailbox, the proprietor is expected to pay various and sundry business taxes in some municipalities. For this reason, many business owners who garner business via mail or telephone, don't display signs, while those who rely on this type of advertising to attract business display them and accept the taxes as a part of doing business. You may think you should call city authorities to find out what you can and cannot do since cities differ in their requirements and restrictions regarding yard signs. Don't. To ask permission is to call attention to your business. Put up a sign if you think it will attract customers. Even though there may be a law that forbids signs, these kinds of laws are rarely enforced. A sign usually goes uncontested if it is discreet. If neighbors protest, then you can change the sign to fulfill legal specifications or pay the fee that is required. Chances are, if you display a sign that is not excessively large or obnoxious, it will not attract the ire of neighbors or the attention of city officials.

Signs can be placed on a variety of surfaces, and certainly any vehicle used for business purposes should bear a sign or two. According to research done by the American Trucking Association, an over-the-road truck makes an average of 10-million visual impressions each year, and a local delivery truck makes 16-million annual impressions. Take advantage of that free publicity. You might place a couple of inexpensive magnetic signs on the family automobile or signs could be painted on it. Magnetic signs can be removed when the vehicle is converted to personal use, although many home business owners happily display business signs at all times. It might be a good idea to have a sign on the vehicle you drive to your primary job because it will attract attention throughout the day and be a good advertising tool. Of course, only do this if there is no competition or conflict of interest between your two occupations and your employer doesn't object.

If your home is located on a busy street, take advantage of the location by placing signs in the yard and on your vehicles for effective after-hours advertising. Flood the signs with light after sunset, and park the vehicles where they are readily visible to passing traffic.

Whether a sign is planted in your front yard, painted on the back of your car or truck, or dangles from your mailbox, the message should be simple and brief with key words in large, easy-to-read print. A sign should not only state the business name but also indicate the kind of work performed. If the sign is on a vehicle, it should include an address and telephone number. A well-designed logo, catchy slogan, or a striking illustration will attract attention and cause the message to be remembered. Recently, while driving behind a plumber's truck, I noticed the phrase, "In our business a flush is better than a full house." This sort of message will attract business because it's hard to forget. The same slogan or logo used on business signs should be included in the telephone directory advertisement. That may be all an individual remembers when they turn to the directory to look for the business number.

A sign's design plays an important role in creating a business image. The style or format should be appropriate for the business it advertises, and it shouldn't appear cluttered or unprofessional. Use the same style on every sign or advertisement to reinforce the image and message you hope to project.

A business name sewn on clothing is another way to capture attention and is an effective way to reinforce a business name. The name could be embroidered on the back of shirts or jackets, on caps, or over shirt pockets. This is especially effective if you go to the homes or offices of potential clients to discuss jobs or give quotes. This is a common practice in construction, repair or delivery businesses but inappropriate for others, especially office-oriented businesses.

The Yellow Pages

Advertising in the Yellow Pages of your local telephone directory is the most practical way to target and attract customers. People look in the Yellow Pages when they have specific needs, and many businesses acquire all of their customers through this mode of advertising. Nordhaus Research of Southfield, Michigan, has shown that 94 percent of adults refer to the Yellow Pages, and each year 83 percent of them either call or visit a business they locate through this source. Unlike the signs discussed above, Yellow Pages advertisements should be chock-full of information because people look at them to learn who does what. Someone repairing small engines should list all the brands serviced, and a photographer will attract more business by mentioning the types of events covered, such as weddings, reunions, and dances. Since you will be working during the off hours, be sure to list your business hours or when your service is available.

Some homes are in out-of-the-way places and difficult to find. If you are located in such a place, it is helpful, when giving clients directions over the phone or when advertising in the Yellow Pages, to mention that you are located "around the corner from so-and-so," or "just a block from (some well-known location.)"

Even if you don't have a business phone line, you can make your name stand out on the white pages of the directory by having it printed in red or bold black type. Of course, this costs a little extra but may well be worth the extra charge. You might also have your name and telephone number listed in multiple directories, such as those delivered to neighboring communities.

Brochures, Fliers and Business Cards

Brochures, fliers, and business cards can be used to promote a business in numerous ways.

FLIERS AND BROCHURES: Many businesses create some sort of brochure or flier in which their services or products are described. This can be a single page printed in one-color or an elaborate layout in full color on slick paper. The one-page version, sometimes called a "flier," is simpler, far less expensive, and is used most often by home business owners.

The style of a flier or brochure should match the type of business it is promoting. I've seen lawn care advertised on a one-page flier with the message written by hand — probably by the guy who was trying to get a job raking leaves or cutting grass. This presentation is quite adequate for this type of business. On the other hand, someone trying to sell advertising consulting services to another business would need to produce a slick, professional-quality brochure. Whatever the quality may be, a brochure or flier must stand out from the competition, be easy to read, and clearly state what services are available.

It could take awhile to figure out how to present your material in the best way, so when starting business, have a limited number of fliers or brochures printed. If the first run doesn't bring in customers, redesign the material and try again. You will eventually discover what is needed to present a clear picture of the services or products you offer and how to present the material so it attracts customers. See Figure 12.1 on p. 110 for ideas on how to phrase your flier.

FIGURE 12.1: Persuasive Words to Use in Advertisements, Promotional Brochures, and Flyers

Whether the promotional material is simple or fancy, be sure to include words that spark interest. The most persuasive words to use in advertisements and promotional material include:

you	results	health	win	easy
free	proven	love	save	introducing
now	today	new	try	guarantee

Fliers can be placed under windshield wipers, hung on door knobs, and distributed at special events or through other businesses. Many businesses willingly permit others to display fliers if they advertise work that complements their own.

Following are a few examples of how fliers can be used.

> ❯ Place those that advertise boat maintenance, swimming, and skiing lessons at marinas and boat sales outlets.

> ❯ Post advertisements for lawn care or a delivery service at a senior citizen's center.

> ❯ Stuff fliers advertising air-conditioning maintenance between doors in early spring; distribute furnace maintenance fliers in early fall.

> ❯ Notices offering furniture refinishing might be posted at auction houses and used furniture stores.

> ❯ Advertise wallpaper hanging services in businesses that sell wallpaper.

> ❯ Promote music lessons in stores that sell musical instruments and music.

> ❯ Offer tilling services at garden centers.

While fliers might be stuffed under windshield wipers throughout the neighborhood or left anywhere for passersby to pick up, you may want to hand the more expensive brochures directly to clients, leave them when making sales calls, or mail them to prospective customers.

Design your printed material to grab your reader immediately or your mailing will be wasted. Since most people receive so many brochures and catalogs, and decide to keep or toss a piece of mail within a few seconds, your mailing has but a fleeting moment to attract that potential customer.

It's important to create a customized mailing list of those who will receive your brochure. If you are trying to attract the attention of other businesses, study the Yellow Pages of your local directory and ponder the headings as you search for potential customers. Or, if you are trying to appeal to private citizens, look for the characteristic that would attract them to your business. Drive through trailer parks to get addresses if you put roofs on trailers, or if you rebind books, university professors and members of book clubs would make your list. It will take a little detective work to prepare a mailing list, but the value of this list cannot be overstated.

After sending brochures to your targeted mailing list, do follow-up phone calls. These calls will increase interest in your product or service and enable you to reinforce your message, set appointments, or take orders.

BUSINESS CARDS: Business cards are also used to promote businesses. Keep your cards readily available, and hand them out at every opportunity. This is an accepted practice in the business world and one that can bring your business to the attention of many potential customers and suppliers.

Challenge yourself to find creative ways to get your business cards into the hands of qualified prospects. You might hand each person two cards and encourage pass-alongs, or you might enclose your business card when you pay bills. When you give a card, ask for a card. This will help you remember names and the person with whom you are exchanging cards will be more inclined to remember you. You could have cards printed to fit a Rolodex, making the card a business resource rather than a promotional item. This could bring business long after the card is given. Never be without cards to hand out. Too many people store, rather than pass out, their calling cards.

Ask others to distribute cards for you. Many businesses are willing do this, just as they are willing to permit the display of promotional fliers. For instance, a physician might permit cards of home nurses in their waiting room; wedding apparel shops often display the cards of caterers, musicians, and printers. As long as you don't directly compete, related businesses will probably display your cards.

Place cards on bulletin boards. Many malls, grocery stores, auction houses, repair and parts companies have bulletin boards for this purpose.

These are but a few examples of the ways printed material can be used to attract business.

Word-of-Mouth Promotion

A satisfied customer is a delight, and a talkative satisfied customer can be a great boon to your business. The recommendation of a satisfied customer is the best free promotion you can get. The best way to acquire a satisfied customer is to provide good products and service and hope they will spread the word. Surveys have shown that pleased customers will tell an average of five people about how well they were treated. Of course, the opposite also holds true. Many small businesses have blossomed through the kind words of pleased customers but just as many have folded because disgruntled people spread the word that the work was inferior or the service lacking. It might be a good idea to send thank-you notes to those who have referred clients to you, or mention it when you see your benefactors. This will not go unnoticed and you will probably get another referral from them if the opportunity arises.

Businesses sometimes use former customers to convince prospective customers that their work is reliable. Always ask permission before including someone on a list of references. This approach is particularly effective if you have done work for people who are well known in the community.

Networking and Relationship Marketing

Success can depend not only on what you know, but who you know, because people are more inclined to take business to people they know rather than to total strangers. It follows that the more contacts you make, the more business will come your way. It pays to get acquainted. To take advantage of relationship marketing, broaden your sphere of contacts — more contacts mean more business opportunities. Join a club, coach a team, attend a church, become active in some movement such as the arts, the environment, politics, sports, and so forth. Clubs like the Kiwanis, Optimist, and Civitan identify themselves as social or service organizations, while others, such as Women in Networking and the chamber of commerce acknowledge their purpose is to promote business among its membership. Actually, all of these organizations are used by their membership to build contacts, and business people recognize that the money and time spent participating in them is little more than a business expense. Consequently, the membership fee of many of these types of organizations is a tax deductible business expense, and 50 percent of the cost of meals consumed at the meetings is a legitimate business deduction if business is discussed at the meetings.

People you work with throughout the day are also potential customers. While it wouldn't be wise to spend your work day talking about this great business you have going at home, it wouldn't hurt to let people know about the services you offer. I know a teacher who runs a small craft business from her home. She buys merchandise on consignment and sells it from her home and at fairs. Her best customers are her fellow teachers. Sometimes a colleague will call in a panic, having forgotten to purchase a gift, and she'll select something, wrap it, and take it along as she goes to school. Another acquaintance has built her business by keeping the women in the office where she works supplied with Mary Kay products. She takes orders and brings the skin care and make-up to work, but she is careful to do the necessary transactions before or after business hours. Both she and her co-workers/customers find this to be a satisfying arrangement. Being able to fulfill the needs of co-workers has proven to be an excellent marketing method for both of these ladies.

Family members are another source of business. Large extended families, and the friends of family members, can add a large number of potential customers that may be more receptive to your sales pitch that the general public. You need to be a little cautious when dealing with family members because some of them might expect lower prices and be lax about payment. Consequently, when dealing with family members, remember you are in business to make a profit, so keep your transactions businesslike or you may find yourself caught in an awkward situation.

Name recognition is also important in relationship marketing. Individuals are more likely to take their business to a known name than to an unknown one. Think back over the times you have turned to the Yellow Pages to locate a business. While working through a maze of business names, weren't you more inclined to stop at one you recognized than at those unfamiliar to you? For this reason, it's wise to get your name before the buying public. Take on an issue, write letters to the editor — do what is needed to get your name recognized. Not only will this effort pay dividends to your business, but it also will be of value to your community.

Don't forget to take advantage of the relationship you have established with past and current customers. Keep them aware of your presence and the services or products you offer. Whether they are down the street or across town, a simple mailer will reinforce your message and nurture your relationship with these customers. In a sense, you can make a sales call for the cost of a postage stamp and a computer-generated printed page, thus saving time and travel expenses while bringing your message to your customers.

Relationship marketing can be applied to each type of relationship you have. For instance, many home businesses have successfully built their clientele by servicing a neighborhood. A truck in the driveway with a business name and phone number clearly displayed is a good way to get started. Looking out my home office window, I see the truck of a heating and air conditioning repair service. This business has been built exclusively through neighborhood referrals. Not only do the neighbors call on this man but, because he offers prompt, good service at a reasonable cost, the neighbors have given his name to friends and relatives who also rely on him. This is relationship marketing at its best. The only advertising needed to keep this man busy are post cards sent to existing customers in the spring and the fall when it's time to have furnaces or air conditioners serviced.

By calling on friends, customers, neighbors, family, club associates, and other relationships, you can keep a steady stream of customers knocking at your door. Tips in Figure 12.2 will help you use your relationships to your best advantage.

Talk Yourself Into Business

Giving talks is an effective way to get your name before the buying public. You may be apprehensive about your skills as a speaker, but you will quickly discover most audiences don't expect a professional performance; they want to learn something and be empowered by your talk. You may have to solicit your first lecture. If you belong to a club or professional association, contact the program director and offer to talk at one of the meetings. Once you have given a lecture, you can be sure you'll be asked to speak to other groups because organizations are always looking for speakers for their meetings.

FIGURE 12.2: Networking Tips

Your goal, when gathering with other business people, is to make contacts that can bring you business. Keep the following networking tips in mind.

> ❭ Start conversations. Be enthusiastic.
>
> ❭ Meet and talk with as many people as possible.
>
> ❭ Give business cards to new acquaintances; ask for their cards.
>
> ❭ Keep track of new contacts; make follow-up calls.
>
> ❭ Always send a thank you note to anyone who sends you business.
>
> ❭ When possible, give a referral to another business — you can expect the same.

You may wonder who would be interested in anything you have to say. Well, for starters, if you decorate cakes, home and entertaining clubs would be an outlet; a lecture by one who prepares taxes would be of interest to any number of groups — especially to people who work at home; a stained-glass artist might be asked to demonstrate the craft to craft groups; a florist might demonstrate making arrangements to garden clubs — and so forth. These lectures would be an opportunity to promote a business. The tax preparer can show how to save money by deftly moving numbers and taking advantage of legal loopholes — and pick up some customers in the process. A stained-glass artist can, while demonstrating the craft, mention that classes are offered and indicate when the next class will begin. Once an individual signs up for a class, they will buy supplies. The amount of money a single student can bring in is surprising. The same holds true for floral design. A florist can expect to sell flowers for use in arrangements. Most clubs offer speakers a small stipend for delivering a lecture, maybe $50, so even if you strike out and don't attract business each time you deliver a lecture, the time spent on the talk won't be totally without compensation.

Workshops and participation in community events are also effective ways to attract free publicity. Many cities offer classes and activities free to the public, and participation can help build your customer base. A nurse whose business is home care could become more visible by offering free blood pressure readings at a shopping mall; or a small business consultant could offer classes in starting a business. Of course, the time you can devote to this type of marketing will be limited since you will be working another job during the day, but until your business is well-established, doing this type of marketing is certainly time well spent.

Media Opportunities

You can use the local media to promote your business either through free publicity or paid advertisements.

Attracting Free Media Coverage

Some people are masters at promoting themselves, and they know how to milk the media for a great deal of free publicity. By using a little ingenuity, you can pick up an interview on television or in the newspapers. Once a story is published, other media become interested. I recently did an article for *Income Opportunities*, a national magazine, about a business in my home town. There had been a brief story about the business in the local press and the proprietor sent a copy of the article to the editor of *Income Opportunities*. The editor realized the story would be appropriate for the magazine and called me to do an interview and write the story. (I'm a "stringer" for several national magazines and regularly write articles for them.) This type of exposure is worth many thousands of dollars to the business being covered.

It's not difficult to pick up interviews with reporters for use on radio, television, or in newspapers. Usually, it's just a matter of letting a reporter know your story would be of interest to the paper's audience. If you provide the reporter with a good lead, or better still a well-organized news release that can be printed without an undue amount of work on the editor's part, chances are, your story will get some press. Much of what you see in the evening news or read in newspapers comes from press releases. The nurse who offers free blood pressure readings would probably have no problem getting a story in the local papers or on radio and television. Of course, a mention of her private nursing business would creep into the story.

Anything that might interest the public will attract the media. If you can't think of how your business is newsworthy, you might send a news release prior to National Small Business Week, which is a nationally recognized week in early May. Explain how home businesses are becoming

---

FIGURE 12.3: Elements to Include in a Press Release

1. Print press releases on letterhead stationery.

2. On the top left, write either "For Immediate Release," or "For "Release After ... and include date."

3. Limit the release to one page; it must contain newsworthy information.

4. Start with a headline that sums up the release.

5. Make the opening sentence enticing enough that the reader will scan the entire page.

6. The body of the release should pique the reader's interest, with the most important information in the first couple of paragraphs.

7. At the end of the story, and set apart from the story, write; "For further information, contact ...." and include your name, address and telephone number.

8. Send photos if they are relevant. Clear, 8 x 10" glossy, black and white shots are preferred.

Editors receive many press releases and won't spend much time evaluating yours. Be clear and straight forward. While you want to catch an editor's attention, you don't want the release to sound like a lot of hype; keep it professional, yet give it an edge so it can compete with the many others the editor receives.

the wave of the future and how your business is impacting your community. Chances are, you'll get your moment in the limelight.

The format for a press release is quite specific, consisting of seven elements, as described in Figure 12.3. It should include a newsworthy item such as announcing a new service, results of research, or something about your business that is unusual or of interest to the general public.

Paid Advertisements in the Local Media Attract Customers

It pays to advertise. Inexperienced entrepreneurs tend to think of their advertising budget as a luxury, and when business is slow, the advertising budget is the first to be cut. But, it's during the slow periods that more, not fewer, customers are needed.

An advertising and promotional campaign should be part of your business strategy. It should not only tell people that you are in business, but it should explain what you offer and show how they can benefit by doing business with you. Although you may get some free publicity now and then, it is necessary to pay for advertisements if you want to have an ongoing promotion that keeps your business before the public.

Advertising through the printed page is usually more economical than radio or television and is the medium used most frequently by home businesses.

A newspaper advertisement can either be a classified listing or a display ad. Classifieds are much less expensive, and therefore more accessible to most home businesses. Classified advertising can effectively target an audience. For example, someone who does hauling might place a classified ad in the "Furniture for Sale" section, or someone who prepares resumes might advertise in the "Jobs" section. The point is, the ad must be placed in the section or category where the target customers are most likely to see it.

Display ads are more visual than classified ads and are especially effective if an illustration is used to carry the message. Certain types of businesses rely exclusively on display ads to draw customers. While display ads cost more than classifieds, long-running ads cost considerably less per printing than those published one or two times.

A display ad should provide the following information.

-) The business name and the type of product or service being offered should be the most prominent part of the ad.

-) An illustration of the product or service will reinforce the verbal message.

-) The business address and telephone number should also be included and, since your hours will not be normal business hours, be sure to state when you are open for business.

Always use the same format and, over time, viewers will associate the format with the message. You can design your own display ads or hire freelancers to do this for you.

Spots on radio and television can also get your business before the public. These are usually produced by the stations that carry the advertisement, although there are many variations to this arrangement. Spots on radio and television are only effective if they are repeated over and over again. Few home businesses use television promotions because they are rather expensive, but the cost of radio promotions are within the budget of many home businesses and are an effective way to advertise. Call your local stations to learn the specifics of such a campaign if advertising through these media appeals to you.

Promotional Gifts Foster Business

Gifts are used in the business world to reward, recognize, and thank customers, and remind them that you are still open for business. According to *Incentive Marketing* magazine, about 50 million business gifts with a total value exceeding $1 billion dollars are given in a typical December holiday season. Promotional gifts to customers are usually designed to remind the customer of the business that sent the gift, and if possible, keep reminding them as the gift is used.

A whole industry has been built around producing and distributing promotional gift items. These items have business names imprinted on them and function as advertisements as well as gifts. The most widely distributed promotional gifts include calendars, pencils, matchbooks, desk pads, key chains, letter openers, and coffee mugs. How many times have you glanced at the pencil you were using or at a matchbook found in your pocket and reflected on when you got it? These articles are doing their job — reminding you of the business that provided them.

You might want to give nonpromotional gifts to your best customers simply as a sign of appreciation. Don't overspend. A gift of small monetary value can be received with pleasure and without the feeling of, "Gads, I owe this guy something!" Last Christmas, a young advertising consultant, who works out of her home, wanted to recognize her customers and decided to give them home-baked cookies. Not having time to bake them herself, she purchased $60 worth of cookies from another home business and placed them on small festive trays. She hand delivered each tray of cookies, giving her a chance to reinforce her presence without asking for an order. Even so, while delivering the small remembrances, she received orders from several customers that more than paid for the cookies and the time spent delivering them. This gift was inexpensive, didn't have the slightest hint of promotion, and came across as a sincere gesture of goodwill and appreciation. It was a perfect gift that seemed to complement the image this very successful lady projects.

It's worth noting that a gift to others is a gift to yourself or your business because the cost of business gifts is a tax deductible business expense.

Finding Customers Everywhere

The two techniques used most frequently to attract customers scattered over large areas are called "direct-mail advertising" and "two-step marketing." Direct-mail advertising involves identifying and mailing advertisements directly to potential customers. This type of promotion was touched on briefly in the previous section but will be elaborated on here because, while it is sometimes used to promote businesses locally, it is more commonly used when campaigns are directed to widely scattered markets. Two-step marketing consists of reaching customers through advertisements in the media and then sending information to those who respond to the advertisement.

Is it more cost-effective to purchase mailing lists and send brochures and catalogs to targeted individuals in a direct-mail campaign, or is it wiser to solicit business through advertisements in printed media such as newspapers, tabloids, and magazines and send material to those who respond to the ads in a two-step campaign? The answer depends on several factors, the most important being, 1) the type of merchandise being sold and, 2) how accurately the market can be targeted. The following descriptions should enable you to select the method most suitable for your business.

Direct Mail Advertising

Direct mail advertising is the most expensive type of advertisement but it is also the one most preferred by major mail order companies. The problem with direct mail is that a large number of companies are using the same selling technique, and this has caused households and businesses to be inundated with piles of brochures and catalogs arriving through the mail. Many of these mailings are discarded without being opened. Each discarded catalog cost somebody some money. A simple, rather commonplace mailing costs at least $.50 and a catalog or brochure printed in color on slick paper could cost several dollars if we include the cost of printing, mailing list rental, mailing preparation, and postage.

The response to a direct-mail campaign depends on how accurately the recipients are targeted. Generally, on a first mailing, a response of three to four percent is considered good. Let's see what that means in dollars and cents. You can expect 300 to 400 of the recipients to respond if 10,000 brochures are mailed. Is the response worth the cost of the mailing?

You can figure the cost of each response very easily. If the mailing was a simple one costing only $.50 each, and 10,000 pieces were mailed, the cost of the mailing was $5,000. If 400 responses (four percent) were received, the cost of each response was a hefty $12.50 ($5,000 divided by 400 = $12.50). But, it may be worth the cost if the respondents order goods that more than cover this cost. To cover this expense and break even, the price of items ordered would have to total at least $25.00. This would cover the cost of advertising ($12.50) and the cost of the merchandise because a $25.00 item would normally cost the merchandiser around $12.50. More expensive items sold by this method would yield a profit. Obviously, this is not a good method to sell inexpensive merchandise unless multiple items are purchased, which is frequently the case when a mailing consists of a catalog advertising many products rather than a flier advertising a single product. The above calculations are based on the response rate you might expect when trying to sell to people whose names were supplied through a mailing list company and with whom you had no prior contact.

Computerized mailing lists with as few as 200 names can be purchased, but usually a business buys at least a couple thousand names for each mailing. Names of businesses cost approximately $60 per 1,000 ($.06 per name and address,) and residential lists cost around $45 per 1,000 ($.041/2 per name and address.) A business might be categorized as to the number of employees, type of sales, amount of sales, and geographical region. Residential listings are categorized as to home owners or renters, age of residents, income brackets, and numerous special characteristics. These lists are so fine-tuned that you can locate just about any segment of the population including art collectors, book buyers, home business entrepreneurs, students, fat people, skinny people, tall people, left-handed people, people with hearing disorders, and so forth. You can request that a list be limited to those within a category but confined to certain geographical areas. Of course, by targeting the correct list, response percentages will increase and money will not be wasted on mailings to those who have no conceivable interest in your product or service.

Theoretically, lists sold by mailing-list houses are updated regularly but some companies more aggressively update their lists than others.

FIGURE 12.4: Tips for Writing Effective Direct Mail Copy

1. Write copy that is personalized and targeted to a specific audience. Think about what audience members want to know. Write copy to answer their questions.

2. Simple copy works best. Short words, sentences, and paragraphs have the greatest appeal. Don't use too many words.

3. The first sentence must grab the readers; they will continue reading only if the first line interests them.

4. Design the copy creatively. Use subheads, underline words, add color, capitalize words, and above all, use print that is large and easy to read.

5. Use facts and figures. Produce believable copy by including statistics, performance figures, names, dates, quotes from experts, and so on.

6. Offer a guarantee. A money-back guarantee will increase response rates.

7. Ask for an order. Provide prospects with an order form, telephone number, and address to facilitate ordering.

Catalogs are still being sent to my home that are addressed to the former resident, who moved away eleven years ago! So much for updating lists.

Names and addresses are supplied on mailing labels or they can be purchased on diskettes, in which case, you print your own labels. Some direct-mail companies will handle the complete procedure, from printing the material to be mailed, to folding and inserting it into envelopes, metering, and mailing. Others supply only the list of names and addresses.

Companies selling lists are located throughout the country. You might start by looking in the Yellow Pages where most likely you will discover large listing companies that have 800 numbers. These companies usually offer free brochures that explain the process of purchasing and using mailing lists. Call for copies of the brochures if you are considering this type of advertising.

With a little effort on your part, you can create your own customized mailing list. With each mailing you will discover people interested in your product or service and from this information you can develop a customized mailing list. Customized lists are invaluable because their use will increase the rate of response, and this, in turn, causes the cost per response to decrease.

A customized list should certainly include current and elapsed customers. Current customers are usually the most receptive to new mailings, and you can expect more orders from them. Mailings to elapsed customers also can bring rich rewards. You can also build a customized list by soliciting the help of current customers. Include a few lines on your order form where customers can list the names and addresses of people who might like to receive a mailing. Figure 12.4 offers some tips for writing effective direct mail copy.

RESOURCE: *Complete Direct Marketing Source Book*, Kremer, 1992, Wiley.

Two-Step Marketing

The first step in two-step marketing is placing advertisements in publications, on E-mail, radio, or television. The purpose of these ads is to interest people in your product or service and entice them to request more information. The second step is sending promotional material to the respondents and asking for an order. Two-step advertising is probably the most cost-effective way to bring in business.

STEP ONE OF TWO-STEP MARKETING: placing advertisements in national publications and via e-mail. Few home businesses, especially those operated as secondary businesses, can support an advertising campaign through national radio or television, but many of them advertise in newspapers, trade, and specialty magazines. Some of these publications have limited circulations, but because they are directed to the group of people most likely to use the service or product advertised, they are effective advertising outlets.

Where should you place advertisements? The first job, when preparing a two-step marketing campaign, is to locate the appropriate publications in which to advertise. There are several directories that list thousands of publications. Of these, *Gale Directory of Publications* is probably the most useful. All directories include publications directed to diverse groups such as farmers, students, collectors of every type, brides, retirees, quilters, auto enthusiasts, and so forth. Ask a librarian for help in locating the type of publications you seek. The directories will indicate the circulation of each publication and the addresses of the publishers. Write or phone (if there is an 800 number) the publications you are considering as possible places to advertise and ask for a rate sheet, a media kit, and a sample copy of the publication. You will receive a profile of the readership, the number of readers, demographics of the readership, a printed form explaining the various rates for display and classified ads, as well as a schedule of due dates. You will quickly discover that the cost of advertising in large national magazines is prohibitive, but advertising in specialty or trade magazines may be well within your reach. These are good places to hawk wares.

After identifying the publications most suitable to promote your business, you are ready to concentrate on the type of advertisements to use. The purpose of the advertisement is to get readers to request information.

CLASSIFIED AND DISPLAY ADVERTISEMENTS: The same options exist for advertising in the national media as in your local media. Classified ads are the type used most frequently by home businesses because they are inexpensive and can accurately target potential customers.

A classified ad in a national magazine with a large circulation might cost $10 or more per word, but it might cost as little as $.20 per word in a specialty magazine or newspaper with a small circulation. Thus, a classified ad reading, "Quilt patterns and supplies; write Granny's Nook, P.O. Box 24, Cranbury, NJ 08512" would cost just a couple of dollars in a small circulation newspaper or magazine but over a $100 in a magazine that is widely distributed.

An ad in a magazine with a small circulation could bring in as much business as one in a magazine with a huge circulation because the response depends on how accurately the readership has been targeted. For instance, the ad offering quilt supplies would attract a lot of interest if placed in something like *Quilt World*, but the same ad, if placed in a magazine such as *Fisherman's World*, would probably go unnoticed.

Display ads in magazines cost considerably more than classified ads, but they are usually more effective. Display ads for publications distributed nationally should contain the same information as those discussed earlier for local publications (see page 118). When using them to attract customers from distant areas, an 800 telephone number will greatly increase the number of responses.

ADVERTISING VIA E-MAIL: A powerful new tool, the computer-driven Internet is vastly increasing marketing and advertising capabilities, and many businesses are using the Internet to market and sell their products. Instead of placing ads in national publications, they advertise on e-mail, sometimes called E-Mall. E-mail is the transmission of messages from computer to computer. It can happen over thousands of miles and across many time zones. All you need is a computer, a modem, and compatible software. Modems are usually packaged with software and information about various e-mail systems.

In the last couple of years, e-mail has seen an explosion of services and networks, making it both a simple and economical method to advertise. You can open a store on the Net by leasing space in a cyber-mall, and the electronic addresses are easy for customers to locate as they "surf the Net." A six-month lease for sending electronic brochures costs around $250; an interactive storefront would cost around $3,000, in addition to set-up fees. Messages on the E-Mall travel the computer network and reach throughout the world. Call the telephone service or computer service in your community to learn more about this far-reaching advertising option.

RESOURCES: *Making Money on the Internet*, Alfred Glossbrenner, 1995, TAB Books.

How to Grow Your Business on the Internet, Vince Emery, 1996, Coriolis Group.

STEP TWO IN TWO-STEP MARKETING: The second part of the two-step marketing process comes into play after you get a response from people interested in receiving more information. Your task now is to send specific product details to turn this interest into a sale. The information you send may be in the form of a flier, brochure, or catalog. An order blank should be included with your mailing. Design the material so it is easy to read and understand, and easy to order. Remember, people who respond to your advertisement have shown an interest in your product or service, so everything you send should be designed to induce them to place an order.

Creating an Advertising Budget

Learning how much to spend and how to use advertising money is a big challenge for new business owners. Yes, advertising costs money, but it usually determines whether or not a business attracts enough customers to make a profit. Spend what it takes to attract customers, but only if sales to those customers bring in enough money to pay for the advertising and generate a profit.

Plan your advertising budget carefully. You may be thinking, "How much can I afford to spend?" The right question is, "How much can I afford not to spend?" because your advertising budget will directly affect the amount of business you generate.

Your promotional campaign will cost much more if you enlist the help of a professional advertising agency rather than doing the work yourself. While professional agencies certainly have more experience and a better feel for how to conduct a campaign, many home business owners do a better job than the professionals because they are more attuned to the way their businesses can affect others. You may need help occasionally, but plan to do the bulk of the work yourself.

The most important concept to carry through your promotional campaign is that promoting a business is an ongoing process, and it is necessary to build an advertising budget into your financial plan. Don't expect to start with a bang. It takes time and money to discover the best promotional techniques and your first efforts might not yield the anticipated response, so don't blow your budget with a splashy all-out campaign. Instead, try different approaches, putting a little money into several different advertising methods to learn which will yield the best response and produce the largest number of customers.

How much money should you put at risk? One approach is to determine the cost of different promotional tactics and work backwards. If it costs a given amount to advertise in a certain way, and this route seems to have the best chance of success, then that is how much should be spent even if the money must be borrowed (within reason, of course).

This chapter has explained that developing a promotional campaign can involve a variety of techniques. You may have noticed that many of the techniques cost nothing — giving talks, networking, word-of-mouth, sending news releases — yet they are just as successful in getting a business before the public as the costly ones. Still, both paid and free promotions are needed if you expect to maintain a public awareness and keep customers beating a path to your door. You should plan your marketing strategy accordingly. But, while you may use signs, Yellow Pages, advertisements, and numerous other promotional techniques, don't forget that people do business with people. Make sure the techniques you use to attract business include a human element because the success of your business rests on your ability to touch, influence, or persuade interested individuals and convert them into paying customers.

RESOURCES: *Advertising for a Small Business Made Simple*, Bernard Ryan, 1996, Doubleday.

How to Make Yourself Famous: Secrets of a Professional Publicist, Gloria Michels, 1994, Hastings.

How-to Book of Advertising: Creating It, Preparing It, Presenting It, Leonard Strong, 1990, Fairchild.

How to Market Your Business: An Introduction to Tools and Tactics for Marketing Your Business, Ian Rosengarten, 1995, Small Business Sourcebooks.

How to Promote, Publicize and Advertise Your Growing Business, Kim Baker, 1992, Wiley.

How to Advertise a Small Business: Step by Step Guide to Business Success, Jerre Lewis and Leslie Renn, 1996, Lewis Renn.

Other Marketing Techniques

HAND CRAFTED AND MANUFACTURED ITEMS ARE produced by many home workers, but business success depends not only on the quality of the work but also on how effectively the products are marketed. There are many ways to get crafted and manufactured products before customers and it is important to select the most cost-effective and productive outlet.

Merchandise can be sold directly to consumers at retail prices or it can be sold at wholesale prices to intermediaries, who, in turn, sell it to consumers. Retailing your own products will enable you to retain all of the money paid for the items whereas you will receive only a portion of the price if others sell your products. The most common outlets for items produced by home workers include art and craft fairs, catalog houses, retail shops, and the government.

Retailing Art and Crafted Articles at Fairs

Art and craft fairs are the only outlets used by many home craftspeople, some of whom have mastered the process of locating the best shows, packing and unpacking their wares, setting up attractive display booths, and bringing in the sales. There is definitely a skill to selling at art and craft fairs and making them profitable and enjoyable adventures.

Some craftspeople work full-time at their businesses, spending weekdays making articles and weekends traveling the fair circuit selling their products. If you are considering a craft business, and expect to sell your merchandise at fairs, you will probably need to modify that schedule due to the demands of your primary occupation. You might consider selling only during part of the year, maybe during the months prior to Christmas, which are the most lucrative for this type of business, and spend the rest of the year building stock.

It's important to evaluate and select the best fairs to attend. Some attract artists and craftspeople who make many items from one or two patterns. Buyers and browsers who attend these fairs tend to go for the "country look" and don't expect to pay too much for the items they purchase. Other fairs attract participants who create original arts and crafts. These fairs are usually juried, which means artists or craftspeople must be selected by a judge before their work can appear in the show. These shows attract buyers willing to pay the higher prices original compositions bring.

Crafts can also be sold at flea markets. I used to counsel craftspeople to avoid flea markets but I have seen these events lure many customers, prompting me to change my advice. While flea markets attract displayers trying to sell imported goods, collectibles, and "junque," there is still room for craftspeople and their wares. In fact, crafts can be sold just about anywhere people gather.

It is important to evaluate your work and decide where it will receive the best response; that is, where you can make the most sales. Attend fairs in your area and talk to exhibitors to learn which fairs are the most profitable, and contact your state arts commission or local chamber of commerce for a list of nearby fairs and shows.

To help decide if a fair is right for your work and worth the time, money, and effort to attend, consider the following points.

1. Attendance. Look for shows that consistently bring in large crowds. A first-time show may not be as profitable as those that are well-established. Show promoters will indicate the number who have attended in past years.

2. Facilities. Is the fair located in a mall, convention hall or other indoor facility or will it be outdoors in a park or on a walkway? If it is outdoors, will you be under an awning or trees, or in direct sunlight? Is there an alternate location if the weather turns bad? If not, is there a rain date? Are tables, chairs, and electricity provided? How large is the booth space?

3. Distance. How far is the fair from your home? Many fairs are Saturday and Sunday events. Will you be away overnight, and if so, can you stay in a camper or will you need to pay for lodging? Maybe it's close enough to go home in the evening and return the next day. Is there security during the night or must you pack up everything and set up your display again the next morning?

4. Time of year. Many fairs are held in spring and summer. These fairs are not as profitable for exhibitors as those held in late fall or early winter when people are thinking about the gift-giving season of mid-winter.

5. Cost. The cost of attending an art and craft fair will depend on how far you must travel to reach the event, if you must pay for overnight lodging, and the booth fee. Attending some fairs costs more than they bring in while others can yield a handsome profit. Of course, these expenses are 100 percent tax deductible — except for the food bill, which is 50 percent deductible — so keep records and receipts of your expenses.

Listed below are things you should do after deciding to participate in a fair.

1. Send in the application form with your booth fee.

2. Make overnight arrangements, if necessary.

3. Build an inventory so you will have enough merchandise to make the outing worthwhile. Design products with the type of gathering in mind. Unless you are attending a juried show, don't expect to sell expensive or abstract art. Instead, produce moderately-priced items that will appeal to a wider market.

4. Design and build a display booth that can be easily assembled and disassembled. You may not be able to park your vehicle near your assigned area and may need to carry or cart your booth. For this reason, it should break down into a tidy package that can be transported from place to place, yet sturdy enough to withstand a gust of wind. Remember to incorporate peg boards, shelves or other means of displaying goods into the booth design.

5. Make a list of the things you'll need during the fair. These might include a stapler, tape, display booth, a cooler with food and drinks, books to read, supplies (if you intend to craft while selling), change and money box, credit card paraphernalia, sales sheets, bags and

packing material for wrapping the sold merchandise, boxes for carrying merchandise to the fair, calling cards, electrical extension cords, chairs, a blanket, table coverings. If the fair is to held outdoors, take an umbrella and throw in some plastic sheeting to cover your display in the event of rain.

Getting to the fair is just half the battle; you also need to attract potential customers and sell your merchandise. Crowds tend to gather where there is some action, and one way to draw people to your booth is to demonstrate your craft. Talk with the people while they watch you work. The longer someone lingers, the better your chance of making a sale. Of course, someone will need to watch over the merchandise and transact sales while you are crafting and talking with customers. Perhaps your spouse, a friend, or kid would be willing to take over that part of the operation. Sometimes a sale comes after a fair has closed and an attendee has had time to think about where a piece might be used. To increase the chance of after-fair sales, have calling cards or printed fliers available for the interested but not-quite-committed browsers.

RESOURCES: A free list of fairs held throughout the country can be obtained by writing the American Craft Council, 72 Spring Street, New York, NY 10012, 212-274-0630.

You might also subscribe to the bimonthly *National Calendar of Indoor-Outdoor Art Fairs* available for $14 per year from the publisher Henry Niles, 5423 New Haven Avenue, Fort Wayne, Indiana 46803. This publication provides information concerning dates, fees, the type of show, past attendance, and where to acquire more information.

You should also be aware of The American Craft Association, 2510 North 47th Street, Station 4, Boulder, CO 80301, 303-449-2570. This is a trade organization for those who produce and sell crafts, and it provides services to members such as securing inclusion of members' products in trade shows, group insurance rates, and other benefits.

Wholesaling Manufactured or Crafted Merchandise

Catalog Houses

Thousands of catalog companies are seeking merchandise to include in their catalogs, and home workers have discovered these companies are good outlets for the products they craft or manufacture. If you are thinking about selling your goods in this way, you should realize that large quantities might be ordered so you must have the capacity to produce on a large scale. Also, pricing is a big factor to consider as you ponder catalog sales. The markup is usually huge, maybe three to four times your wholesale price, rather than double, as in retail stores. In order to make the merchandise competitive, you may need to lower your wholesale price. This pricing requirement will certainly reduce your profit, and for this reason this outlet may not be desirable. Of course, when your products are distributed through catalog companies you will spend less time and money marketing so perhaps you can take lower prices for your wares.

There is a specific procedure for submitting merchandise to catalog houses, with submission deadlines for each season's entries. Study catalogs and decide which catalog houses seem most appropriate for your merchandise, then write to learn how to submit a proposal. Catalog companies rarely want a sample submitted but prefer a good-quality photograph with a descriptive write-up of each product to be considered. Apply to numerous catalog houses to increase the chance of having your product accepted. However, you should be aware that some catalog houses insist on exclusive rights to a product.

RESOURCES: *Selling to Catalog Houses*, this kit includes a Catalog House directory and 200 Catalog House labels, all for $20 from Success Publishing.

How to Sell Your Product to Mail-Order Houses by the Thousands, Duane Shinn, 1976, Duane Shinn.

Your Own Mail Order Business

Another way to sell merchandise through catalogs and mail order is to create your own catalog business with a catalog of your own products, and sell directly to consumers by direct mail or through advertisements in publications. This should be considered only if you: 1) produce large quantities of merchandise, 2) price the merchandise high enough to cover the cost of producing a catalog and the expense of advertising, and 3) can accurately target potential customers. To reach potential customers you need to acquire appropriate mailing lists or place advertisements in publications targeted to potential customers. See the discussion of mail order businesses in Chapters 2 and 12. Also, refer to the extensive resource list in Chapter 2.

RESOURCES: *Selling Arts and Crafts by Mail Order*, Allen Smith, 1990. Success Publishing.

Catalog Handbook: How to Produce a Successful Mail Order Catalog, James Hollan, 1991, Hippocrene Books.

Retail Stores

Retail shops provide another possible outlet for crafted and home manufactured items. Buyers for retail outlets either purchase the merchandise outright, in which case they pay the wholesale price, usually one-half the retail price, or they stock the merchandise on consignment and pay nothing until the articles are sold. The craftsperson usually receives 60 to 70 percent, rather than 50 percent, of the sale price when articles are consigned because the shop owners don't have money at risk when they stock consigned merchandise. Generally, it's better to sell wholesale to shops rather than have goods placed on consignment but, if a consignment arrangement is the only way to get your merchandise into a store, you might as well give it a try. If the merchandise moves, the buyer will be more inclined to purchase subsequent orders at wholesale prices. To locate outlets for your merchandise, it is necessary to visit retail outlets and show your wares. See "cold-calling," discussed later in this chapter.

Buyers for retail shops also attend trade shows in an effort to locate merchandise. If you can produce large quantities of items, it may be beneficial to display your products at these shows. Display space can be expensive, especially in large shows, and your participation is only cost effective if you can attract enough orders to more than cover this expense. Most trade shows are limited to specific lines of merchandise. Among the many types of shows are those that display only jewelry, computer ware, crafted items, bedding, giftware, farm equipment, and apparel. Some shows are national while others are regional.

RESOURCES: *Creative Cash: How to Sell Your Crafts, Needlework, Designs and Know-how*, Barbara Brabec, 1991, New Careers Center. Ask for a copy of the publisher's free *Whole Work Catalog*.

Selling What You Make: Profit from Your Handicrafts, James Seitz, 1992, TAB Books.

Start and Run a Profitable Craft Business, William Hynes, 1992, Self-Counsel Press.

Tradeshows Worldwide, An International Directory of Events, Facilities and Suppliers, published by Gale Research Company. Published annually.

How to Get the Most Out of Trade Shows, Steve Miller, 1996, NTC Publishing Group.

Sales Calls Bring in Business

Sales calls to potential customers and to well-established ones are a good way to increase sales.

Cold Calling

"Cold calling" means making sales calls to people with whom you have not previously done business. The purpose of cold calling is to attract new customers. It's not among the things we like to do most, but it is on the list of activities that can effectively bring in new business. There is a lot of business waiting to be uncovered and, in many cases, asking for it is all that is needed to make a sale. For this reason, every entrepreneur wanting to increase business should devote time to cold calling. Even when the people you solicit don't have an immediate need for your services or products, your time is well-spent if the potential for future business exists.

There are several methods of cold calling, including door-to-door solicitation, phone prospecting, and calling on "leads" — people you have learned might need your services or product. Some methods are more effective than others.

Door-to-door solicitation means stopping at homes or businesses unannounced in an effort to make a sale. Whether going to each home within a neighborhood or visiting businesses distributed throughout a city, door-to-door solicitation is less successful than the other methods, and it gives the wrong impression. There is a tendency to think salespeople who go door to door have little business and therefore have time to do this time-consuming task. The biggest problem with door-to-door solicitation is the decision maker of the business is rarely available to the salesperson who pops in without an appointment. Also, it's not cost-effective because of the time and expense involved in traveling, whether it's across town or just down the street.

A more effective way to make a cold call is by phone, and the goal of the call is to set an appointment. Business-to-business sales calls don't usually receive the same cold shoulder as the aluminum siding salesperson who gets you out of the shower, but it's still a challenge to get through to the buyer or decision-maker.

When cold-calling another business, treat the gatekeeper with respect, and learn the name of the decision maker before you try to talk business. Getting this information can be a little tricky, but the easiest way is to first phone the company to obtain the name of the decision maker, then call back later to make your sales presentation. Maintain control of the conversation from the beginning. Give your name and the name of the person you are calling because this implies that the party you're calling will recognize your name.

Prior to making the telephone call, prepare prospects by sending the person a letter and a flier or brochure with a description of the products or services you offer. Mention the mailing when you call. Don't rely on your memory to produce a good presentation. Instead, prepare a script or an outline for your telephone conversation. Your script or outline should include an introduction of yourself, your business, and what you can do for the client.

Don't try to sell anything over the phone; just try to get in the door of the prospective customer. With an appointment made, the scene is set for you to make your pitch. According to Gary Goodman in his book, *You Can Sell Anything by Telephone* (Prentice Hall), the phone is the most cost-effective means of selling. Goodman offers some tips on how to encourage potential customers to stay on the line long enough for you to make the point that you understand their needs and can fulfill them. Don't ask your prospect when you can come in for a few minutes, but suggest specific times, like, "I'd like to see you next week. Can we make an appointment for either Tuesday or Thursday?" With an appointment made, get off of the line. Busy people appreciate efficiency.

The most productive cold calls are to people to whom you have been referred. Existing customers can direct you to others needing your services or products, and it's always worth asking clients if they know someone else who can benefit from your services. Sometimes the answer is a list of names and numbers. Making calls to referrals is the easiest type of solicitation, and you should certainly mention that your client suggested you give the individual a call. This immediately gives you and your prospective client a common interest.

Getting leads for phone solicitation is valuable whether you are offering services to businesses or individuals, and the best way to get leads for phone solicitation is to identify sources of information and seek their help. For instance, if you offer pet sitting or other pet services, perhaps you can uncover prospective clients by working through a veterinarian or pet store owner who will give, or sell for a minimal fee, lists of customers. Or, if you offer personal services such as addressing holiday or seasonal event cards or transportation of children of working parents, contact an organization of working women such as Women in Networking or child care centers because they will be working with or for parents who can use your services. A sports instructor might get lists of prospective customers from sports equipment shops, and a supplier of firewood can get leads from businesses that sell wood stoves.

Persistence leads to success. You will be rejected, you can count on that, but keep dialing that phone because there is business to be made. It's just a matter of identifying the people who need your help and offering it to them.

Get into the *habit* of making cold calls. Don't do this type of marketing in bursts when all your other jobs are completed. Instead, take time from your daily schedule to make a few calls and send some letters or brochures to potential customers on a regular basis. This persistence is what is needed to keep bringing in new customers.

Nurture Existing Customers

Strive to strike a balance between searching for new customers and serving old ones. It's unwise to spend time chasing new customers at the expense of old ones. According to Ken Kupper, president of Revelle International, a Miami-based firm specializing in customer care, "Business goes where it is invited and stays where it's appreciated." Customers may stop dealing with a business for various reasons, but seven out of ten customers who have complaints will return to a business if their problems are resolved in their favor.

Customers appreciate a business that follows up a problem with a call to make sure everything has been resolved. It's also a good idea to send thank you notes for past business.

"Regaining a lost customer should be a priority," claims Loren Marc Schmerler, president of Atlanta's Bottom Line Management. If you discover one of your regular customers has stopped bringing you business, call and find out what the problem is. Listen closely to the answer and do what you can to resolve the issue. This personal and caring contact goes a long way in drawing customers back to your business because that customer will feel valued.

Newsletters are a good way to keep in contact with existing customers, and besides helping to improve your professional image, they also function to give your business increased credibility in new markets, promote your product line, and highlight accomplishments or changes. Putting together a newsletter used to be a big chore, but now many computers have desktop publishing capabilities and, after the stories are written, the newsletter can be easily formatted on the computer. Mail newsletters to both established as well as potential customers.

Sales Representatives

Sales representatives (sales reps) can make sales calls for you and get your products on the market because you will probably be too busy with your primary occupation to spend time on the road. Large businesses hire sales reps to sell only their products, but independent sales reps are self-employed and sell merchandise for many manufacturers, some of whom are home-business owners. Most sales reps expect exclusive territory, meaning they are the sole representative of your merchandise in that area. You will need to hire several or many sales reps, each covering a defined geographical area, if you intend to enlarge your range of business. Sales commissions are normally paid monthly and range between 15 and 20 percent of the total sales. To locate sales reps, place advertisements in either craft or trade journals or look in these journals for advertisements from sales reps who are looking for lines to add to their portfolios. Ask for help at your local library as you seek trade journals that are appropriate for your business.

RESOURCE: *How to Build Sales with Manufacturer's Agents*, Jim Gibbons, 1989, Prentice Hall.

Selling to Federal, State, and Local Governments

The government is spending your money but, with a little planning and ingenuity, you can get some of it back through your business.

The Federal Government

The federal government buys more goods and services than any other customer in the free enterprise system, and your chance of being one of its suppliers is just as good as anyone else's. Many small business owners have built successful businesses by selling to the federal government.

In fiscal year 1995, the federal government contracted for over $260 billion worth of goods and services directly from the private sector. The government buys from very large corporations as well as from very small ones. You should consider doing business with the federal government because, while it may be in debt, it pays bills regularly and makes a good customer.

To take advantage of opportunities to sell to the government, you need to know where in the federal structure to make yourself and your products known, how and where to obtain the necessary forms and papers, and how to bid for the opportunity to sell specific goods or services. These procedures and rules are easily managed, and help is available to facilitate the acquisition of contracts by small business people.

Government purchasing agents make an effort to encourage a broad spectrum of the business community to bid on perspective projects. There are special provisions that spread opportunities among all business segments and geographic areas of the country. The chances of small firms are boosted by the efforts of two programs. One is the Business Service Center Program, which offers trained counselors to assist entrepreneurs in their search for government contracts and furnishes step-by-step help with contracting procedures.

The other program that offers help to small businesses is administered by the Small Business Administration (SBA). The SBA works closely with federal purchasing agents to develop policies and procedures that lead to increased contracts being awarded to small businesses. It also provides a wide range of services to help small business owners obtain and carry out government contracts. To locate SBA help, look in your local telephone directory under Small Business Administration or SCORE. If neither is listed, call your local chamber of commerce for directions or call the SBA office in your state capital.

Besides help from government personnel, a computerized system has been instituted by the federal government to aid and assist the small business owner in becoming known to the government as a potential supplier. This system is known as PASS, or Procurement Automated Source System. PASS is a high-tech, computerized network that contains the names of businesses and the goods or services they can provide. If you wish to be considered for federal contracts and subcontracts, simply register your company with PASS. Thereafter, computer identification of your firm is made whenever work of an appropriate nature comes along. You can be listed in the system at no cost.

The Veterans Administration is a branch of the federal government that spends nearly $3 billion each year as it serves over 29 million veterans. It actively solicits small business owners to offer their goods and services for its consideration. For information on how and where to be listed as a supplier to this expanding market, write to the Director, Office of Procurement and Supply (90), Veterans Administration, Washington, DC, 20420. Ask for the publication *How To Do Business With the DVA*, and for information about how to complete a Bidder's Information Form. After filling out the form, you will need to send it, along with catalogs, price lists, and other material about your products or services, to the proper purchasing center. This will place you on the active bidder's list, and you will be informed when the product or service you can provide is needed.

RESOURCES: *Doing Business with the U. S. Government: How to Sell Your Goods and Services to the 200 Billion Dollar Federal Market*, Herman Holtz, 1993, Prima Publishing.

Doing Business with the Federal Government is a valuable resource for learning about selling to the federal government. The booklet costs $2.50 and can be ordered from Consumer Information Center-J, P.O. Box 100, Pueblo, CO 81002.

Your Business and the SBA, a free booklet and a simple-to-fill-out PASS application can be obtained by writing or calling SBA, 1441 L Street NW, Washington, DC 20416, 202-653-8200.

State and Local Governments

Just as the federal government needs services and products, so do state and local governments. While contracts are acquired through bidding, the old-fashioned sales call is also a way to locate business. For instance, if a community has an annual festival, you can be sure the paraphernalia used to promote the festival — hats, pin-on buttons, streamers — comes from local vendors. Political campaigns also bring opportunities for small businesses in the form of promotional sales. Keep alert to local and state happenings and ask for the business.

Tending to Taxes,
Insurance, and Benefits

Taxes and insurance don't elicit much excitement and no doubt you would just as soon ignore them. But taxes won't go away and insurance is a good policy. Also, one of the advantages of being the boss is you can create your own benefit program. Home workers must deal with each of these issues, but people moonlighting at home will find they are easily managed.

Business Taxes

TAX LAW FOR HOME BUSINESSES IS STRAIGHTFORWARD. Many deductions are allowed, and the process of filing a tax return is less intimidating that you might expect.

Defining Your Business Objectives for the IRS

You must establish that you are engaged in a business, rather than pursuing a hobby, in order to qualify for business deductions. The goal and intent to earn a profit is what distinguishes a business from a hobby. Business profits are taxable income and business losses can be deducted from other earned income. A hobby is an activity without a profit motive. Although profits generated through a hobby are taxable, losses that result from the hobby cannot be deducted from other earned income. You're right, something doesn't seem quite fair about this ruling, but that is, nonetheless, the present situation.

Many home businesses look more like hobbies than businesses. The tax law reads, "If the activity has produced a profit in any three of the preceding five years, it will be presumed to be a business activity." There is confusion about this rule. Many think this means if a loss occurs three out of five years, then the activity is considered to be a hobby, but that is not the case. If an activity produces a loss in three out of five years, it may still be claimed as a business if it is evident that the goal is to earn a profit. The following activities are indicators that the endeavor is a business engaged in earning a profit.

1. The activity is carried out in a businesslike manner, with appropriate records maintained.

2. The services or products are advertised to the public.

3. The activity is operated under a business name.

4. Stationery and business forms are printed.

5. A business plan with goals and projections has been developed.

It is worth creating a paper trail and a business image so there is no question that you are in business and your goal is to earn a profit. Only then will you be allowed to take tax deductions available to business owners.

Meeting Tax Obligations

The government expects you to pay taxes on the profit your home business generates. Income received and expenses incurred as a result of self-employment are reported on Schedule C. In addition to the income tax you must pay, self-employment income is subject to social security tax. The self-employment social security tax is computed on Schedule SE. Most home workers can file the short Schedule SE.

You are required to file quarterly estimated tax payments on the taxable income generated by your home business. Estimated taxes can be filed on Form 1040-ES and are paid in four installments, the first one being due April 15.

Deducting Expenses

You should take all allowable deductions for your home business expenses, as these will significantly reduce your tax liability. It is necessary to identify and document all expenses associated with your business.

Supplies and Equipment

The cost of supplies and equipment used in your business activities are tax deductible expenses. Supplies include printed material and other office supplies, as well as the goods and materials needed to provide a service or produce a product.

More expensive items such as a furniture and office equipment (fax machine, copy machine, and computer) can be expensed. That is, the entire cost of these items can be deducted in the year they are purchased up to a limit set by the IRS. Check the instructions that accompany Tax

Form 4562 to learn how much can be expensed. Another option is depreciating each item, which means you apportion the cost over a period of years. Expensing is almost always preferable to depreciation because, not only is the method simpler, but a tax write off is more valuable the earlier it is used since the money not paid in taxes can be used for other purposes.

You may have numerous others expenses such as advertising and other promotional costs. These, too, are deductible.

Travel, Food, and Entertainment

You can deduct the cost of travel connected with your business. This includes lodging, meals (50 percent of cost) transportation to and from your destination, and reasonable tips.

A vehicle used for business purposes is tax deductible. Tax law requires that you keep a log book in your vehicle and record the mileage and destination each time you make a business-related outing. You can claim mileage costs plus tolls and parking fees. If a vehicle is used only for business purposes, it is not necessary to keep a log because, in this case, all expenses associated with the vehicle are tax deductible. When traveling by rail, bus, ship, or air, retain the tickets for verification.

Fifty percent of the cost of entertaining in the pursuit of business can be deducted as a business expense. This must be an activity that is appropriate and helpful in the conduct of your business. The deductible expenses include meals, beverages, parking, and so on. Use Form 2106 to report these expenses.

Keep two kinds of records of your travel and entertainment expenses — receipts and an expense diary. These are not only needed when filing your tax returns but they are essential in the event your return is audited.

Other Tax Credits

You may need help with your children, a disabled dependent, or with housekeeping chores in order to have time to pursue your moonlighting operation. Are you aware that you can hire child care or care for a disabled dependent, either in your home or away from home, and claim a tax credit for a percentage of the care? A tax credit is subtracted directly from your final tax liability instead of from taxable income, making it more valuable than a deduction of the same amount. The percent you can claim is based on your adjusted gross income (AGI).

A tax credit can also be claimed for the services of a housekeeper. These credits cannot be used if the individual being paid is one of your dependents, but the credit can be claimed if the money is paid to relatives, including your children, if they are age 19 or older. You cannot claim more of a tax credit than you earn. Use Form 2441 to claim the dependent care and household services credit.

Deducting Your Work Space

Perhaps the largest deduction for people who work at home results from the allowances for home work space. These tax breaks are significant and can greatly reduce your tax obligation. Even when a home business brings in only a modest profit, the tax deductions allowed for the use of work space can make operating a home business a valuable asset. The government is lenient with home workers as they get their businesses underway because, if they are successful, they will contribute to the tax base.

Home-use tax deductions include a percentage of the utility expenses (gas, electricity, and water,) mortgage interest, rent, insurance premiums, property taxes, depreciation, casualty losses, security systems, repairs and maintenance costs, cleaning and lawn care costs, and the total amount of money spent developing the area used for the home-based business.

Prior to the tax reform of 1991, the only reference to home work-space expenses was on the "Profit and Loss From Business" line, IRS Form 1040, Schedule C. If you claimed home work-space deductions on Schedule C, it was a well-known fact that your probability of being audited was significantly increased. Many homeworkers elected to forego tax deductions for home work-space in the past because they were frightened by the threat of an audit. The IRS has finally acknowledged that over 25 million people are working from their homes, and home-use deductions are legitimate claims. To facilitate making these claims, Form 8829 has been introduced to be used when calculating home work-space expenses. According to the IRS, Form 8829 is a more accurate way to assure that the amount you claim for home-use work-space deductions will be close to what you're entitled to, and the IRS maintains that using this form will *reduce* the chance of being audited. You might be put off by the need to use another form, but Form 8829 makes it easy to calculate home work-space expenses and serves as a checklist to make sure you declare all the deductions to which you are entitled. The ease in using this form is inducing many home workers, who have been reluctant to claim home work space in the past, to come out of the closet and claim this worthwhile deduction.

Currently business space in the home can be claimed for full-time operations as well as part-time or second-income businesses. You can take a tax deduction for your home work space, even though your main job is away from the home, if the home work-space meets the guidelines established by the IRS. However, you can't deduct your home work-space if it creates a net loss for the business in a given year. The disallowed amount can be carried over to the following year if, again, it does not produce a net loss. There is no time limit on the carryover. Any amounts disallowed can continue to be carried over until there is a net profit from the business against which the expenses can be deducted. This provision has proven to be a windfall for owners of many small businesses that slowly evolve into profitable ventures.

The part of the home used for business purposes must meet certain requirements to qualify for the home-use deductions. It must be:

1. Clearly *separated* from family living space.

2. Used *exclusively* for business purposes.

3. Used on a *regular* basis.

4. Serve as the *principal* place of business. You may work another job, but your home work space must be the principal place of business for your **home** business. **Work space must meet all four of these criteria** before it can be claimed as tax-deductible space.

A free-standing structure, separate from one's dwelling, such as a trailer, barn, or garage, that is used exclusively and regularly for business purposes also qualifies as a tax deductible zone, even if it is not the principle place of business.

The deduction allowed for the business use of one's home is based on the percentage of floor space used for business purposes. The percentage can be figured in either of two ways. The preferred method is to divide the square feet in the home into the number of square feet used for business purposes; thus if, in a 2,000 square-foot home, 500 square feet are converted to business use, then 25 percent of home expenses can be claimed as a tax deduction. The other method for figuring space is to count the number of rooms if they are nearly equal in size, and divide the number of rooms used for business purposes into the total number of rooms. If one room is used in a five-room house, then one-fifth, or 20 percent, of the home expenses are legitimate business deductions. See Figure 14.1 for the kinds of expenses that are tax deductible.

Calculate deductions attributable to business use by multiplying the total home expenses by the percentage of the home floor space used for business purposes. For example, if it costs $5,000 for total home expenses, and ten percent of the home is used for business purposes, you can deduct $500 for the business use of your home. You can also deduct the

---

FIGURE 14.1: Tax Deductible Home Expenses

A portion of the following expenses are tax deductible. The portion that is deductible is relative to the portion of the home claimed for business purposes on your tax form.

- › Rent, if the residence is rented

- › Depreciation, if the residence is owned

- › Mortgage interest

- › Property taxes

- › Insurance premiums

- › Cleaning expenses, including the salary for cleaning person

- › Maintenance costs, including painting, replacing windows, repairing gutters and so forth

- › Extermination and termite inspections

- › Lawn care

- › Utilities, including water, gas, and electricity

- › The total cost of refurbishing or remodeling the area used for business purposes.

entire cost of decorating, painting, or remodeling the portion of the home used for business purposes.

It's advisable to enclose a photograph of your home office and work area with your tax return so the examiner can more fully understand how you are using the space you are claiming as a deduction. This type of documentation goes a long way toward warding off an audit. Refer to IRS publication 587, *Business Use of Your Home,* for instructions when preparing your tax return.

Finding Tax Shelters

One big advantage of operating a business and earning a profit is that you can shelter virtually all of the earnings from income taxes. The principle behind tax-sheltered plans is that money is invested in various securities but taxes on the earnings are deferred until later, when the money is withdrawn. This deferral can result in a huge benefit because of the extra interest earned on the money not taken out in taxes. Some of the more popular tax shelters include IRAs, Keogh Plans, the Defined-Benefit Keogh Plan, annuities, flexible spending accounts, and deferred compensation plans. The advantages and disadvantages of some of these shelters are discussed in the "Retirement" section of the next chapter. Talk with a tax accountant or an estate planner to take advantage of tax shelters.

Keep adequate records to facilitate figuring tax returns and to document expenses should those returns be audited. Good records are an indication that you are truly in business, and the deductions you claim are for legitimate business expenses. Records used to operate your business are adequate for tax purposes. See Chapter 11 for a discussion of bookkeeping and recordkeeping procedures.

IRS Resources

Free publications offering tax advice for home workers are available from the IRS by calling 800-829-4477, by fax 703-487-4160, or by visiting your local IRS office. The following are guides or forms of special interest to home workers.

103 Small Business Tax Education Program (STEP) — Tax help for small businesses

155   List of tax publications, How to order

305   Recordkeeping

355   Estimated tax

407   Business income

408   Sole proprietorship

451   Individual retirement arrangements (IRAs)

454   Tax shelters

509   Business use of home

510   Business use of car

512   Business entertainment expenses

554   Self-employment tax

602   Child and dependent care credit

Schedule C (Form 1040) Profit or Loss from Business (Sole Proprietorship)

Schedule SE, Form 1040 Self-Employment Tax

Form 8829 Expenses for business use of your home

Insurance and Benefits

INSURANCE AGAINST RISKS AND THE BENEFITS you need or want are two issues that require thoughtful attention. Risks will be as much a part of your business life as they are of your personal life and you need to decide how you will deal with them. Benefits normally extended to employees need to be created for the self-employed. If benefits are extended to you through your primary employer, you will not need to create another package for your moonlighting business.

Dealing with Home Business Risks

The financial responsibility for some types of risks can be shifted from your business to an insurance company through insurance policies. A sound insurance protection plan is important to both the security of your business and your personal financial well-being, because without this protection, your business and personal property can be lost and you can be forced into bankruptcy. Being insured against life's many risks is a good policy.

Insurance premiums are the price you pay for the freedom from worry about economic loss from conditions beyond your control. The question you must answer as you develop an insurance package is, "What am I willing to risk?" You should insure what you can't afford to lose. Try to strike a balance as you develop an insurance program. Guard against being insurance poor but also guard against being poor as a result of purchasing too much insurance.

The insurance protection you buy may prove to be one of your most important purchases, and it's worth spending the time and effort it takes to become a knowledgeable consumer. Good insurance management includes identifying insurable risks and locating an insurance representative who will help you obtain adequate insurance coverage at the best price.

Don't rely on standard homeowners' or renters' policies for coverage because most of them are written so as to specifically exclude claims involving business endeavors. In fact, some insurance brokers will not accept home-based businesses for commercial liability policies, while others welcome the opportunity to provide coverage.

The main types of insurance you should consider are discussed in the next section, but there are many others available that may be appropriate for your circumstances.

Basic Coverage

The three main risks faced by home business owners that should be covered by insurance are described below.

1. Liability to the public. Personal liability and product liability are risks that must be protected against. These risks include both personal injury as well as damage to the property of others. Liability insurance is especially important if clients visit, or deliveries are made to your home office. All you need is somebody falling down your porch steps and breaking a leg to put a big hole in your business plans. You must protect against economic ruin from this type of incident. Home owner's or apartment dweller's policies can be broadened to include liability insurance for business purposes. This addition to your policy is called an Incidental Business Option or a Business Pursuits Rider. It will protect you against slip-and-fall lawsuits related to your business, and usually this addition costs very little money. Claims for injuries or damage due to actual rendering of services or the sale of a product are excluded in these additions. You will need a commercial policy for full protection in case your product or service causes injury or damage to the buyer.

   Automobile insurance is another type of liability insurance. When an employee or subcontractor uses a car in your behalf, you are legally liable even though you don't own the vehicle. Risks of this nature can be covered in your auto insurance policy. This is especially important if you employ sales representatives or delivery personnel. The insurance you have on your car probably specifically excludes business-related claims, and you will need to add a rider to cover them.

2. Damage to business property. Inventory and business space are at risk from fire, storms, earthquakes, and other perils, and an insurance policy is needed to protect against their loss. Ask your insurance representative if your home owner's policy covers business losses in your home. If not, you could purchase inventory and equipment insurance but sometimes the most economical way to cover these and other issues associated with your home and business is through an umbrella policy acquired through the same company and at the same time as you obtain your home owner's and auto insurance policy. Considering the litigious nature of the American society, I wouldn't consider operating without this umbrella of protection.

To ensure that you can document losses, keep a detailed list of your home office equipment, furniture, and other valuable business assets. For each item, include the original purchase date, price, and serial number, and place the list in a safe deposit box or safe.

3. Liability to employees. Most home workers don't have employees, but for those who hire helpers, it is necessary to have them covered by insurance. Worker's Compensation Insurance provides funds to cover medical expenses should an employee be injured while working. This type of insurance is required by law in most states. Worker's Disability Insurance, which is rarely required by law, provides employees income in the event they are unable work as a result of a disability incurred on the job.

Specific Coverage

Besides insuring against the three major risks discussed previously, you may want to ask your agent about the following kinds of insurance, but remember, the agent is anxious to sell as much insurance as possible, so carefully evaluate the risks against the policy costs.

Business Interruption Insurance covers fixed expenses that continue if a fire or other disaster disrupts or closes your business. You probably won't need this type of insurance, because not only are the expenses of part-time home businesses usually minimal, they can probably be covered by income from your primary occupation.

You might also consider insurance to cover Excessive Loss From Bad Debts and Crime Insurance, which covers loss due to burglary, robbery, disappearance of money and securities, and vandalism. Be sure to discuss the various types of coverage with your agent while preparing your insurance program.

Bonding

Any service that presents a significant risk to a client or the client's property should be bonded. Being "bonded" means insurance is carried against damages or losses that result from services performed. This is essentially a form of liability insurance that assures customers that, should a loss occur, it can be recovered. A bonded service should be identified as such in advertisements because many people are reluctant to engage unbonded workers or service providers.

Finding an Agent

You will need the help of a qualified agent, broker, or consultant to explain options and recommend the right coverage. If possible, consult an independent insurance agent because, unlike agents who represent a single insurance company, an independent agent can pick and choose from numerous companies to put together a package that best fits your needs.

Before accepting any policy, read and understand the fine print and know exactly what the policy covers, although you won't really know until you have a loss. Keep all insurance records and policies in a safe place, preferably in a safe deposit box. If you keep the policies at home for convenience, then keep the policy numbers and insurance company's name in your deposit box or give them to your accountant or a family member that does not live with you.

There is the misconception that insurance costs are nearly the same among the different insurance companies, but equivalent policies can vary significantly from company to company, so shop around to find the best offer. Also, take advantage of special proposals. Some companies offer discounts if smoke alarms, fire extinguishers, and deadbolt locks are used, and may offer a reduced rate on automobile insurance to those with good driving records.

After your insurance program is in place, you may discover a better arrangement with another company and will want to switch companies to take advantage of this. You can cancel a policy at any time and be refunded a portion of the premium. While you might do this occasionally, don't make a habit of jumping from company to company. Also, insurance companies can cancel with a five-day written notice. This sometimes happens when too many claims are made and the insured party is considered to be a poor insurance risk.

Review your policies periodically to make certain the coverage is adequate and your premiums are as low as possible while giving sound protection. Don't try to save money by underinsuring because you think the probability of loss is small. If the probability of loss is small, the premium will also be small.

Common Sense Protection

There are many ways to protect your home and business that don't require paying an insurance premium. A few risks, and ways to guard against them, are listed below.

1. Protect against fire damage by placing fire extinguishers in selected spots. Periodically check that they are operating properly.

2. Install smoke detectors at strategic locations throughout your home and business area.

3. Store flammable materials in closed containers and place them in a cool area.

4. Practice good housekeeping and don't allow trash to accumulate.

5. Install pin-tumbler cylinder locks in all doors.

6. Install an alarm system. Perhaps the family dog can alert you to intruders.

7. Keep monies and important papers in a high quality, fire resistant safe that is secured to the floor.

8. Have adequate indoor and outdoor lighting for night protection.

9. Keep all keys under your care; issue as few as possible.

10. Place convex wall mirrors or two-way mirrors in the shop, if appropriate.

11. Leave the cash drawer empty and open at night.

12. Remove excess cash from the cash drawer and place it in a safe place.

13. Keep complete inventory records and check for irregularities.

14. Sign all checks yourself.

15. Review all canceled checks and their endorsements.

RESOURCE: *How to Protect Your Home from Burglary and Fire*, 1991, Gordon Press. This excellent book costs $79.95, but another book, also titled *How to Protect Your Home from Burglary and Fire*, Louis Hobson, 1982, is available for $3 from Sunnyvale Press.

Creating a Benefits Package

Employers normally offer benefits to their employees, some of which are required by law, and may include insurance coverage for health, disability, and death, along with options to buy stock at reduced prices, paid vacation and sick days, educational opportunities, and retirement programs. You will not need to develop a benefits package if your primary occupation offers a comprehensive package, but if benefits are not provided, you should create a benefits package through your home business.

Health and Life Insurance

You will need to purchase health insurance until some form of comprehensive public health insurance becomes a reality.

Locating an affordable and adequate health insurance plan is becoming increasingly difficult but it is not impossible. Health insurance can be purchased individually or as a participant in a group policy. Group policies designed for the self-employed often have higher limits and more benefits than individual plans. Also, there is a better chance you will be able to purchase coverage at a better price if you are a part of a group than if you try to acquire it individually.

Life insurance is also included in benefits offered by many employers, with the employee and the employer each contributing a percentage of the premiums. Again, if this is not covered through your primary occupation, it is essential that you purchase life insurance. Besides protecting your family, an adequate life insurance policy is required should you need to borrow a large amount of money to develop your business.

To learn what insurance plans are available to you and at what cost, consult an independent insurance agent. Also, write to several of the organizations for the self-employed listed at the end of this chapter to learn of the benefits and insurance plans available. The main purpose of these organizations is to gain bargaining power and lower prices for their members.

Plan for Retirement

Like other working Americans, you must contribute to the Social Security program. This is done through your primary occupation each time your are paid and through your home business each time you make an estimated tax payment to the Federal Government. Even though you are contributing to your Social Security account, you should realize that Social Security payments made to you during retirement are not designed to provide the "good life." Their purpose is to supply money for food, shelter, and basic needs. If you want to assure yourself of a more gracious retirement, pay into a retirement plan that you develop now with the provider of your choice. Many retirement plans are available to the self-employed. Several were briefly mentioned in the last chapter as tax shelters but it's worth taking a closer look at some of these plans, so if you aren't covered through your primary occupation, you can set up a program that will afford you a comfortable retirement.

The most popular retirement plan is the individual retirement account (IRA), which allows you to shelter up to $2,000 each year in a tax deferred account. People below certain income levels, and not covered by other qualified retirement plans, can deduct their IRA contribution from their current year's taxes. Even if you exceed the stated salary requirements, and cannot deduct the contribution from your taxes, the shelter is valuable because interest earnings on the contribution are deferred until they are withdrawn. The tax deduction privilege changes from time to time, depending on the persuasion of our elected officials.

You might consider a Simplified Employee Pension plan (SEP). SEPs are the easiest of qualified plans to manage and they are also the most flexible. To participate in the plan, simply open an account with a qualified custodian, usually a bank, brokerage firm, or mutual fund company, and contribute up to a maximum of 13 to 15 percent of your income. (This rate changes so check with the custodian of the account for the latest figure.) Each year or month you can add to the account or open new ones.

Even bigger contributions can be put into a Keogh plan, especially the Defined-Benefit Keogh plan where, under certain circumstances, 100 percent of your self-employment earnings can be invested. These plans are considerably more complicated to organize and administer, but if you are bringing in sufficient income and want to shelter a large portion of it from taxation, a Keogh plan or a Defined-Benefit Keogh plan could be your best option. Money invested in these programs compounds tax-free until it is withdrawn which makes it a very good investment.

As you establish a retirement plan, remember penalties are usually assessed for early withdrawals. While some plans allow you to borrow funds before retirement age for medical expenses and other valid emergencies, others do not. Call your financial planner to get the facts straight and for advice about retirement planning.

Some retirement plans are available through support organizations for the self-employed (listed below), while others can be secured through banks and other financial institutions.

Bargains for the Self-Employed

There is strength in numbers and there is bargaining power as well. Support groups for the self-employed have been formed to take advantage of this bargaining power and, as a result, they offer good buys and substantial discounts on health and dental insurance, prescription drugs, rental cars, lodging at hotels and motels, new cars, auto repairs, and long-distance telephone charges. They also offer services such as travel arrangements, newsletters, business conferences, and many others. Some of these organizations publish catalogs listing the benefits available. It's worth investigating the groups and studying their catalogs to determine if they can be of value to you. A few of the more prominent groups are listed below.

American Small Business Association. 206 East College Street, Grapevine, TX, 76051. 150,000 members.

National Association for the Self-Employed. P.O. Box 612067, DFW Airport, TX, 75261-2067. 300,000+ members.

National Small Business Benefits Association. 2244 North Grand Avenue, East, Springfield, IL, 62702. 39,000 members.

Small Business Service Bureau. 554 Main Street, P.O. Box 1441, Worcester, MA, 01601-1441. 38,000 members.

RESOURCE: See the annual *Encyclopedia of Associations*, published by Gale Research, for a comprehensive list of organizations directed to the self-employed. This publication is available in many libraries.

Taking Control of Your Life and Your Business

Your business success will depend upon the wise use of your time and energy. Time management will enable you to use these valuable assets to the best advantage. Starting a business is one thing, but managing it well and making it thrive requires continuous review and dedication. While working toward business success, also strive for success in your personal life because only when you achieve a balance between your business, family, and friends will you experience true contentment.

Time Management:
What You Really Need to Know

TIME MANAGEMENT IS THE KEY TO ORGANIZING your life and work and getting jobs done in a timely fashion. Don't underestimate the value of structuring your time and setting boundaries for work and play. You will not be able to do all you would like or need to do, so be prepared to set priorities and delegate responsibilities. It's up to you to set the pace and build a multifaceted life, but you also must know your capacity and set limits.

Focusing on Work

Being your own boss requires a type of self-discipline and motivation that isn't required when working for someone else. It is important to give extra attention to developing good habits, self-discipline, and self-motivation because a lack of these characteristics can sabotage your business. Keep in mind that determination is the key to success; a quitter never wins and a winner never quits.

Incorporate time management principles into your work day. Don't meander between jobs or waste time on activities that don't contribute to your success. Watch for lost moments, whether they are spent in idle chatter or in nonproductive work. While working at home, you'll be close to a lot of possible diversions including the television, refrigerator, family, and bed, and it's very easy to get pulled away from your work. Sometimes you will be tired and want to take a nap long before chores are completed, but if you want your dreams to come true, don't oversleep. Each time you resist a temptation, you build resolve and it will be easier to resist the next time you are tempted.

You also need to know when to stop working. Work without end is work without joy, and it is very easy to slip into the habit of working and

FIGURE 16.1: Tips for Improving Your Time Management Skills

Organize

) Keep files current and color-coded. Separate papers into "active" and "inactive" groups. Use colored folders to help you quickly locate frequently used documents.

) Clean off your desk. This will save time sorting through piles of papers.

) Create new files for things that clutter your desk — items you need, but don't need close at hand — news clippings, reference material, and so forth.

Prioritize

) Make a schedule and number the jobs in the order they should be accomplished. Then execute each task in order of priority.

) Use high energy time to tackle difficult jobs; do the work you enjoy most during your waning hours.

) Keep notes. Don't expect to remember dates and facts. Use a calendar to keep track of deadlines, schedules, I and events.

Be in Control

) Say "No," and mean it.

) When interrupted, don't hesitate to tell callers you are busy, and the same goes for visitors who arrive without notice. Offer to return calls or reschedule visits at a more convenient time.

) Call back. Set aside a regular time to make and receive calls. After awhile, clients, family, and friends will become accustomed to your schedule.

) Start fresh. Take a few minutes at the end of work to throw away trash and file papers.

) Invest in yourself. Take advantage of high-tech equipment and services that can save you time, such as modems, fax machines, computer programs, voice mail, and so forth.

) Screen calls. Use caller ID to identify callers. This puts you in control, allowing you to answer only those calls you deem worthy of your time.

) Do two things at once. Use headsets or a cordless phone so you can file, type, open mail, or other simple tasks while talking on the phone.

ignoring other important parts of your life. Since your moonlighting job will probably start late in the day, you may have a tendency to work late into the night. That is not the answer unless you can function with little sleep. It may take longer to accomplish business success if you work only three to four hours each night, but it is unwise to think you can do much more than that. Of course, you may need to work into the wee hours sometimes, but it's not a good idea to make this a normal routine or your health will suffer. Figure 16.1 offers some tips for improving your time management skills.

Organizing and Planning

One thing you can't recycle is wasted time. To ensure that you don't waste this valuable asset, make time management a part of your work routine by following goal-oriented schedules and by planning ahead.

Schedules are simply a way to plan your work. Planning puts you in control of your business rather than being controlled by it. Schedules can help you forge past interruptions and concentrate on the chores at hand.

For each work session, it is wise to make a schedule and list the jobs to be done. This list should be written down and prioritized. Number the tasks in their order of importance and work through the list, crossing off each job as it is completed. If, at the end of the work period, some chores have not been finished, then move them to the top of the list for the following day. If these tasks aren't done the following day, they must be low priority and you might eliminate them from future schedules. Written schedules will enable you to jump start each work session, eliminating the problem some people have of wasting time as they try to get their work day underway.

Schedule errands and do multiple errands on each outing. It's a good idea to make a list of the various places you must go and arrange them in an order that ensures you don't backtrack.

Try to keep to your schedule and avoid management by crisis because it wastes valuable time and diverts you from your priorities. A crisis is an unexpected interruption from the normal course of events that is so important that you have little choice but to stop what you're doing and tend to the crisis. Overcommitment is the source of the great majority of crises so it is prudent not to attempt more than you can accomplish.

Planning will prevent many crises or at least limit their consequences. By anticipating things that might go wrong, you can prevent them from happening, saving time and interruptions. One of the easiest ways to prevent a crisis from occurring is to be sensitive to how your business is operating and catch a crisis before it materializes. If you are to complete a project on a given date, it's a good idea to plan the work so it is finished before that time. This will allow time to work out problems, should they occur. I do this every time I write a book. After agreeing with my editor on a completion date, I schedule when each chapter must be finished, leaving time for a rewrite and a little writer's block.

Make sure a crisis is indeed a crisis before you forsake other tasks and move into a crisis management mode. People tend to think every little problem is a crisis, but more often than not, many problems will resolve themselves without intervention. Learn to recognize when you need to step in to settle a problem or step aside and let the matter resolve itself.

Striking a Balance

You are about to undertake the biggest balancing act you have ever attempted. You will need to juggle two jobs while finding time for family, friends, fun, and yourself. It's essential that you learn to strike a balance between your many roles if you are to make a life while making a living.

The most important thing to remember, as you strive for balance in your life, is you must control your schedule rather than allow others to take control. Only you know how much time can be devoted to various activities.

If you have trouble separating different aspects of your life, or if the people who share your life aren't sure which mode you are in, try wearing different wardrobes for your different roles. As soon as you return from your primary occupation, dress either for your moonlighting job or for the role you play as friend, spouse, or parent. This will enable you and the people around you to understand how to interact, and you will be more inclined to be immersed in the role at hand.

Train your family. Interruptions cost time and money. Of course, you will want and need to spend time with your children and spouse but it is necessary to set limits. When you are working and can't be interrupted, close the door to your office or shop. Make your family understand that they can only interrupt in the case of an emergency — and define emergencies.

Be sure to keep your family apprised of your activities and tell them what you're working on. After all, your spouse and children may not think of their house as a place of business, so it may help if you explain what you're doing and why. If you must work extra hours to finish a big project or get ahead for a vacation, talk about it. It's important for your family to understand your need to work.

Bring your friends into the loop. They, too, need to be aware of your time limitations so, together, you can plan time and activities that are fun and fulfilling.

Don't forget to save some moments for yourself. Admittedly, this will be difficult, but everybody needs time to reflect, soak, read, and hang out now and then.

Managing Child Care

The demands of your business may not allow you to care for children during working hours. According to a survey by the SBA, at least 40 percent of the mothers working at home do not care for their children while working. Christine Davidson, in her book *Staying Home Instead*, estimates the amount of time you can concentrate on work when children are around. Her estimates are: from birth to four months, zero hours; from four months to 18 months, one to two hours a day; from 18 months to three years, two to four hours a day; from three to five years, four hours; and school age, five to eight hours a day.

If you need more time to concentrate on work, consider hiring a babysitter, or ask an older child, grandparent, friend, or neighbor for help. Expect to pay helpers; remember, part of the money you pay for child care can be used as a tax credit. Of course, your spouse might be willing to provide the help you need, and this could be the best arrangement for the children.

When possible, take a child along on short trips or when running errands. Spending even small amounts of time with a child can reap big dividends in building a healthy relationship.

If you must find child care outside of your home, look for a center nearby, as this will allow easier access to your child, and less time will be spent in transit to and from the care center.

It will be a challenge if you must care for children while running your business, but planning will help ease the conflict. Separate work activities into those that require quiet time and those that do not. Arrange work around your children's schedules, so nap time, feeding, or play time can be put to good use. Handle important calls or meetings during nap time or when your home is most tranquil, but use time when the children are fretting or roughhousing to file papers or do less demanding work; it's virtually impossible to do much thinking when children are noisy.

You might arrange to have your child work alongside you. Anne Williams, of southern Indiana, has found her six-year-old son enjoys working with crayons, paste, and a host of other art supplies. She has incorporated a desk for the child into her office and keeps a large container under the desk filled with art supplies. She tosses in new articles regularly — from pieces of string to empty T-paper rolls — and her son spends hours converting the supplies into art objects, gifts, and toys. All the while, Anne is able to stay on the job while keeping an eye on her youngster.

Avoiding Time Wasters

You can get more for your time by working smarter, not harder. Look for ways to save time. For instance, keep equipment and tools in place so you don't need to search for them each time they are needed.

Routines save time and can be very productive. Build routines into your work day because they will allow you to get jobs done in a methodical, systematic manner that leaves little room for indecision and lost moments.

When possible, do two things at once, whether it's talking on the phone while putting stamps on envelopes or preparing a box for shipment while something is being faxed or printed.

Get into the habit of making decisions rather than procrastinating and putting them off until later. Indecision requires you to rehandle papers and rethink issues — and that takes time.

Learn to say "No." You will need to get into the habit of saying "No" to the many requests that come your way — from church suppers that need servers, scout troops that need leaders, school events that need chaperons — and the many other requests that can consume time. It's not fair to expect others to always do the work, but you will have little time to spare and must be very selective when participating in non-business activities.

During work time, beware of the drop-in visitor or the neighbor who doesn't have much to do and wants to spend the evening chatting. Friends are a delight but they can squander your time. Let friends and neighbors know your schedule and that they must not interrupt unless in an emergency.

Meetings are sometimes necessary but you might get more done in less time if you mix business with pleasure. Try scheduling business meetings over dinner or an early breakfast — perhaps before heading out to your day job.

Making Your Telephone Work for You

A telephone can be your biggest time saver or your biggest time waster. Following are a few tips on how to use your telephone to save time and energy.

Never go shopping without first calling to learn if the item or service you are seeking is available. When you locate the item, ask the cost and determine when the store or shop is open for business. This will save you countless hours and considerable energy going from store to store.

A major time waster for many people is simply talking too much. Whether talking on the phone or over the back fence, learn to keep conversations short. Limit the length of telephone calls with a timer. Whether you are returning a call or picking up a ringing phone, determine immediately if the call will be completed within a reasonable time, and if not, set the timer. I keep a timer on my desk for those callers who don't get down to business. I'll give them a couple of moments, set the timer, and when it rings (it can be heard over the phone), say the timer has rung and I must be excused. No lie, just a little sidestepping.

You can easily screen calls with an answering machine or a caller ID apparatus. This will enable you to pick up desired calls but leave others unanswered. It is unwise to inform friends and family that you use a caller ID device because they will wonder if you are avoiding them when you fail to answer the phone.

Businesses are built on information. You need information to be successful and much of it is available by phone for free or for very little money. Matthew Lesko, author of *Lesko's Info-Power* (Info USA), writes, "The American government is the biggest source of information in the world, and it's all accessible to anyone with a telephone." His book is crammed with names and numbers of people who can answer questions, send you material, and guide you to more resources.

Getting information takes patience and persistence. It takes an average of seven calls to locate the information you are seeking. Just accept the telephone run-around as normal and stick with it. Once you locate the right experts, you need to inspire them to share their expertise with you.

Of course, getting information by phone may sometimes require long-distance tolls, but gaining information through the phone is a fast, inexpensive method of conducting research.

Combining the power of a computer with the power of a telephone line enhances our ability to gather information even more. The Internet enables home workers to tap into vast stores of information and bring it, via the telephone line, to their computer screens.

Streamlining Paperwork

Handle each piece of paper only one time. In other words, make a decision and act accordingly — either toss, file, or respond.

The average worker spends nearly three hours each week just handling papers. You will be working part-time so you can expect to spend considerably less. Still, to reduce time spent doing paperwork, simplify your office. Clear your desk of extraneous papers and make it a work space, not a storage area. Keep close at hand only what you consistently need and use, for example, a telephone, answering machine, stapler, and scotch tape.

Don't allow papers to pile up. Make sure you have adequate storage and filing space, and set aside regular work time for filing. Clean files and desk drawers every six months, or so, discarding what's not current. Some experts suggest this basic paperwork rule-of-thumb: if the thought of throwing out a certain document creates anxiety, keep it. Otherwise, throw it out.

In an effort to cut down on paper clutter, store as much information as possible on your computer — lists, names, orders, and invoices — but keep your calendar and day's schedule on paper so you can refer to it frequently as you make appointments and plan your work through the day.

If you have a problem discarding magazines because they contain some good articles that you've not gotten around to reading, keep in mind that, as much as you would like to, you can't read everything. By the time you get around to the stockpiled publications, much of the information may be outdated. If you see an article you really must read, tear it out, place it in a rack by your toilet, and toss the magazine. Keep magazines you receive to a minimum by evaluating each subscription before renewing it. If a magazine does not add to your business or personal life, don't renew.

RESOURCE: *Taming the Paper Tiger*, Barbara Hemphill, 1995, Kiplinger Books.

Staying Motivated and Fighting Burnout

It is important to stay motivated as you strive to run a successful home-based business. Home-workers must create for themselves the reinforcement and support that employees get at work. While striving to stay motivated, you will also be vulnerable to burnout because you will be working two jobs — and you will be working while other people play. Burnout is the feeling of discouragement and being bogged down. According to Dr. Beverly Potter, psychologist and author of *Beating Job Burnout* (Ronin,) "Burnout is a process in which motivation is damaged by feelings of powerlessness." This feeling can arise from several causes, particularly isolation, working long hours, a sense of being trapped in your own work, lack of recognition from peers, and lack of appreciation from others.

The way to stay motivated and fight burnout is to develop the "I can do" spirit and recognize and enjoy your successes. Too many people work day after day, but fail to recognize little accomplishments along the way.

Remind yourself of the rewards of working at home. You are your own boss, can work at your own pace, and set reasonable goals and standards.

Also, mix short- and long-range goals. Meeting daily or weekly objectives offers an immediate reward. It's hard to sustain long-term projects without this type of reinforcement.

When you find yourself fighting to keep at it, divide your work into jobs you enjoy and those you'd rather not do. First do the unpleasant tasks and then reward yourself with one you enjoy. By doing this no work period becomes pure drudgery.

Maybe you should join a small business club or support group. Besides being a good way to network, these organizations can keep you motivated and help you shrug off burnout. They also are a good way to learn about new technologies, changes in tax law, and other business-related issues. But, a word of caution, while the sharing of business experiences is important, you must be very careful when selecting an organization, and limit your participation.

Avoiding that Stressed Out Feeling

Stress is normal. Expect it. Everyone experiences stress at one time or another, and you can count on a little extra dose because you will have an extra load to carry.

People respond differently to stress. Some thrive on it and are bored when there isn't a lot of action around them, while others become overwrought when there is too much to do and not enough time to do it. Watch for the following stress signals.

> ❭ Feeling overwhelmed
> ❭ Feeling out of control
> ❭ Feeling bored, loss of purpose
> ❭ Headaches
> ❭ Moodiness
> ❭ Sleeplessness
> ❭ Lower back pain
> ❭ Stomach disorders
> ❭ Consuming more drugs including alcohol, nicotine, and caffeine

Managing stress is the best way to cope with the problem. This may mean learning new skills to help you accomplish more in less time and thereby circumventing stressful moments, or it may require organizing your work so you aren't confronted with deadlines. Try to avoid getting in the position that too much is required of you. For instance, if your busiest period is during the holidays, do as much as possible in anticipation of the heavy work load, plan to put in long hours, and keep in mind the season will pass and you can return to behaving like a normal person again.

Goals can set you up for stress. If you expect to accomplish more than is reasonably possible, change your goals and make them more realistic. Your physical condition can also affect how you handle stress. Learn to relax, and seek serenity in your work. Practice breathing deeply, and follow an exercise program that forces the stress out of your pores.

RESOURCE: *Simplify Your Life: One Hundred Ways to Slow Down and Enjoy the Things That Really Matter*, Elaine St. James, 1994, Hyperion.

Stress Management Strategies, Glenn Schiraldi, 1994, Kendall-Hunt.

Time Management Made Easy, Peter Turla, 1994, NAL-Dutton.

You Can Find More Time For Yourself Every Day, Stephanie Culp, 1995, Betterway.

....

Growing Your Business

IT'S ONE THING TO START A BUSINESS BUT QUITE another to make it thrive and grow. Early this spring, while walking in a field and kicking the stubble left behind from last season's harvest, I realized home workers have a lot in common with farmers. Since farming is the leading home business, it's not surprising the two groups share common goals and practice similar business procedures. Both cultivate their businesses and reap what they sow. And, while they must tend to daily chores, they must constantly lay the groundwork for the future, by cultivating new business, and plowing some profit back into the venture.

It might be instructive to think about the many ways you can increase the fertility of your field of customers, bring in a healthy crop, and increase your profits.

Lay the groundwork. Farmers till the soil each spring in anticipation of the upcoming planting season. They are planning for the future. You also need to make business plans, turning over each idea until it is well-worked.

Plant seeds of interest. Seeds must be planted in order to harvest a crop. Make an ongoing effort to plant seeds of interest in your business through a diversity of marketing techniques.

Harvest the crop. After planting seeds of interest, be prepared to nurture potential customers and reap sales.

Weed out unproductive lines and services. Some of the projects you try may fail to bring in much profit. When it becomes apparent that a part of your business is unprofitable, don't hesitate to yank it out and strive to make a more productive line take root.

Glean the fields. Did you miss something? It's always a good idea to take a second look at your business to make sure you aren't missing a good opportunity.

Mend fences. Successful entrepreneurs tend to fences so customers don't stray to competing businesses. This ongoing process is well worth the effort it takes, because past customers are the easiest to attract for future business. If a customer has a problem, make every effort to rectify the problem and that customer can be counted on for more business.

Milk the cow for all it's worth! Take advantage of the producing stock and nourish it so it continues to yield profits for your business. At the same time, always watch for stronger lines and use them to expand and strengthen your productive lines.

Cultivate a new field. You will generate more sales and earn more profit if you attract more customers. Always look for ways to expand your client list.

Plow profits back into your business. You will surely take some of the profit your business generates as payment for your labors, but it is wise to use most of the profit to solidify the financial foundation of your business.

And now, let's get a little more specific...

Review Your Business

Are you satisfied with the way your business is operating? If not, how will you change your approach to be more successful? Periodically reviewing past performance is helpful, but the most effective way to keep your business functioning at maximum efficiency is to make review and evaluation a continuous process. By constantly monitoring your business operation, you can intercept problems before they cause much damage and capitalize on good directions and increase profits.

Don't expect continuous success without setbacks. There could be many months when you don't fulfill expectations but that doesn't mean you have failed. Businesses respond to economic, seasonal, and cultural cycles and you can expect your sales and profits to reflect these cycles. For this reason, compare sale figures for comparable periods and look for trends rather than sales within a short period.

The most important part of evaluating your past performance is identifying which parts of your business are most profitable and which are least profitable. Many entrepreneurs are surprised, when they finally sit down and study their profit and loss records, to learn that something they had considered to be the backbone of their business does, in fact, take a lot of time and effort but yields very little profit, while another, less obvious part of their business, is quite profitable.

Have you checked your business plan lately? You probably started off with a plan but it may have gotten lost in the shuffle. Take a look at your plan to see if you are still on track. Or, maybe you need to adjust your plan to reflect changes in the market. A business plan should never be cast in stone so it can be changed as conditions change.

Have you kept apprised of your competition? While you don't want to become consumed by competitors' activities, it's worth keeping an eye on them. Borrow the ideas or methods that seem better than what you have been using.

Are you sensitive to the market? Do you watch for changes in customer needs? Customer satisfaction is essential for the growth of your business.

How are your finances doing? You will know if you adequately estimated start-up and operating costs after you are in business for awhile. Are your operating expenses about in line with your estimates?

Refine Goals

Take another look at your goals. If you fail to meet goals in a timely fashion, analyze why you missed the work. Don't look for excuses but look for reasons. If your old goals fall short, don't be afraid to create new goals that will redirect your energy. Successful businesses regularly redefine goals, whether the economy is booming or whimpering. They also respond quickly to changes in the marketplace and look for ways to adapt to these changes. If you focus on growth, not survival, on long-term prospects, not on short-term losses, and on new solutions rather than old problems, you will develop the strategies needed to grow.

It may take more than refined goals and a renewed commitment to keep your business current and competitive. Perhaps you have noticed how quickly the business world changes. Make an effort to keep current and up-to-date. Keep apprised of new products based on emerging technologies that may affect the way you do business. It's hard to keep up with the array of new equipment available to home workers, but some of it can make such a difference in work efficiency that you should watch for new products or techniques.

Manage Growth

Business growth depends on many factors — but most of all it depends on your drive and determination, and your ability to position your business, to be creative and take advantage of new opportunities.

Cultivating certain personal qualities will help your business thrive. These qualities include flexibility, tenacity, and prudent spending.

> › Flexibility. As the economy changes, the needs of customers change, and you must adjust your business accordingly.

> › Tenacity. You will experience tough times and must be prepared to meet them head on. Just keep plugging away. Your business will make it if your plans are solid and administered properly.

> › Prudent spending. Draw a minimal salary and keep purchases to a minimum while income is slow. Plan ahead for expenses and don't plan expansions or extra projects until you see the momentum returning to your business.

Make sure you are getting the most from every dollar, whether it is spent for advertising and promotion or for finding the best supplier at the lowest cost.

As you grow your business, don't be tempted to expand through inappropriate diversification. Diversification that requires too much outside labor or financial commitment could be debilitating to your existing business. Make sure the new avenues you pursue strengthen those already in place.

Create a balance between the amount of business you can bring in and the stress and time it demands. More is not always better, and you will need to be sensitive to the point when your business has reached its optimum size. At this point, replace lost customers with new ones, but don't try to expand your customer base.

Keeping the Profit Motive

Profit is what business is all about. Continuously fine tune your business in an effort to increase profits. Look for ways to cut expenses without cutting services because profit is directly affected by the cost of doing business. Profit is what's left over after expenses are deducted from income, so any change in either income or expenses affects the amount of profit. Profit can be increased in several ways.

1. Sales increase but costs rise at a slower rate.

2. Sales remain constant but costs are cut.

3. Sales increase while costs decrease.

By making accurate observations about your business and reacting in positive ways, you can make one of these profitable scenarios — preferably number three (increasing sales while decreasing costs) — happen.

Question the way you do business as you look for ways to increase profit. Can you find materials and supplies at lower prices? Is there a cheaper way to ship? Should you have minimum orders? Do you spend money too freely? Do you have too many outstanding bills? Are your credit checks adequate? Is too much money tied up in inventory? Is your product or service competitive? Have you sought customers' suggestions? Is there a better way to market your business? Is there a more cost-effective way to deliver your service? Is there a quicker way to get a job done? What other questions are appropriate for your business?

Remain alert to changes in tax laws that may affect your business, and adjust work space to take full advantage of tax breaks available to home workers.

Save money and increase profits through the conservative use of supplies. Watch for ways to save on electricity and other utilities. For instance, don't leave your printer on all day but turn it on only when documents need to be printed. If possible, wait and print everything at one time so the machine does not need to be turned on and off too often.

Use rechargeable batteries if you use portable equipment that requires batteries. It costs more to get set up, but it won't take long to recover the cost and start saving money.

Electronic mail may help save a few bucks. MCI Mail's Preferred Pricing option allows you to send up to 40 e-mail or fax messages for $10 a month. Is there a better deal out there? There are many money-saving techniques and it is worth pursuing them.

Avoiding Common Mistakes

Small businesses fail for a variety of reasons. Some of the most common mistakes that contribute to failure are listed below.

> Getting into the wrong business. This sounds obvious but many businesses fail either because the owner lacks the background needed to run the business effectively or because there are too few potential customers to produce an adequate number of sales.

> Starting out undercapitalized. Most small businesses don't make a profit immediately so the new owner must be able to draw on other resources until money starts flowing into the business.

> Neglecting the business. An owner makes or breaks a small business and is required to wear many hats to make the business succeed.

> Failing to have an adequate plan. The need for a business plan cannot be overemphasized — it keeps you on course.

> Expanding too fast. Small businesses must expand carefully, making sure sales justify the expense of expanding.

> Poor service. Small businesses must take special care to offer excellent service and foster good customer relations.

> Relying on one or two major clients. Landing a large client is good for business but a diverse client base offers more security than a few large customers.

> Undercharging or overcharging. Charge what the market will bear, but keep in mind that sales will be lost if prices are too high.

> Handling complicated business matters alone. Hiring a lawyer, accountant, ad agency, or business consultant may be expensive, but sometimes the expertise of a professional can save you money. Know when it's time to hire professional help.

> Taking growth for granted. Customers are a perishable commodity. Don't be content with last month's sales, but keep looking for new customers even when business is great.

Measuring and Enjoying Success

It's important to recognize and celebrate successes. Develop your own definition of success. Others may think driving an expensive new car indicates success but you may recognize success as a trend of improved sales or acquiring a skill that was difficult to master.

Your attitude will influence how successful you feel. Think and talk positively about your business. Accentuate the positive and give an upbeat report on your business when friends ask about it. You've probably heard the expression, "Success breeds success." It seems that the belief in success also breeds success. When you talk about how well your business is doing, family and friends will pick up on this, and before long you will find yourself puffing up a little and feeling very good about yourself and your business. You have every reason to feel good because, to quote Christopher Morley, "There is only one success — to spend your life in your own way." Your way is owning and operating your own business. Enjoy!

Business Opportunities
You Can Pursue from Home

HERE IS A LIST OF NEARLY 500 OCCUPATIONS that can be developed at home. In compiling the list, special consideration was given to occupations that will fit into crowded schedules and limited space and will work nicely as secondary businesses. The income one might earn from the various occupations ranges from quite small to very large.

As you study this list and consider what job might be best for you, think about how much time you can devote to your moonlighting job, and assess your abilities, interests, equipment, experiences, and space. Keep in mind whether this work is something you will be doing in off seasons (as farmers and teachers might), or if you will work at your home business after putting in a full day at another job.

Try to select an occupation that will complement your primary employment. If you work throughout the day doing heavy labor, maybe your second occupation should be more sedentary or, if you sit at a desk most of the day, you might prefer a second occupation that involves physical effort. If your primary job is mentally demanding, consider a second career that requires less mental activity, and so forth. You may want to take advantage of the skills you use in your primary job to develop a second income, thus the work you do at night will be similar to the work you do during the day, except you're the boss. Do you want to be surrounded by family and friends when you are working? Keep in mind that some occupations require quiet so you can concentrate while others can be done while in the midst of the hubbub of family life.

Some of the occupations listed below require little background while others are based on experiences and education; still others require physical agility or sheer strength. Special attention is given to the many occupations that can be accomplished at home because of the new tools that have become available, affordable, and user-friendly in the last few years. Computers, fax machines, and other high-tech equipment allow home workers to be a part of the information economy because they can be electronically linked to the larger business world. Many technology-driven occupations are especially suited for evening work.

All of the jobs listed below can be based in the home. Jobs like delivery or a cleaning service require the work to be done elsewhere while occupations such as accounting or computer programming can be accomplished at home.

The occupations are listed alphabetically and, when available, references are provided. For further reading, see *The Best Home Businesses for the '90s* by Paul and Sarah Edwards, 1991, Tarcher. This book lists many of the most workable home businesses, and includes the earning potential for each and the skills and background needed to be successful.

Another good book on this subject is, *101 Businesses You Can Start From Home*, 1995, Wiley. Also, you might refer to *The Best Nonfranchise Business Opportunities*, Sherman, 1993, Henry Holt, or one of the many books listing business opportunities to be found in your local library.

Accountant: *How to Run Your Business with the Home Accountant*, Elizabeth Hulsizer, 1986, Prentice Hall; *Accountant's Business Manual*, William Behrenfeld and Andrew Biebl, American Institute CPA; *How to Start and Manage an Accounting Service Business*, Jerre Lewis and Leslie Renn, 1995, Lewis Renn.

Acting: *Acting as a Business; Strategies for Success*, Brian O'Neil, 1993, Heinemann.

Addressing service: *Envelope Addressing as a Small Business: A Business Workbook*, Data Notes Publishing Staff, 1991, Prosperity and Profits.

Advertising agent: *How to Build a Small Advertising Agency and Run It at a Profit*, Len Gross and John Stirling, 1984, Kenwood; *Advertising Realities: A Practical Guide to Agency Management*, Wes Perrin, 1991, Mayfield Publishing.

Advertising specialties sales: *Advertising Specialty*, Guide Number N1292, Entrepreneur.

Advisor in your area of expertise: *Advice, a High Profit Business: A Guide to Consultants and Other Entrepreneurs*, Herman Holtz, 1986, Prentice-Hall.

Aerobics and exercise instructor: *Exercise Senior Style: Guide for Instructors*, Susan Malmstadt and Marilynn Freier, 1993, Cottonwood Press; *Aerobic Dance: Handbook*, J. Jackson, 1992, Kendall-Hunt.

Air-brushing: *How to Airbrush T-Shirts and Other Clothing*, Diana Martin and Ed Martin, 1994, North Light Books.

Air conditioner installation and maintenance: *Air Conditioning, Fundamentals of Service*, Staff, 1994, Deere and Company.

Alarm systems installation and maintenance: *Security Distributing and Marketing* Magazine, 1350 East Touhy Avenue, Des Plaines, IL, 60018, (312) 635-8800; *Alarm, Sensor and Security Circuit Cookbook*, Thomas Petruzellis, 1993, TAB Books.

Alterations: *Sewing for Profit*, Judith and Allan Smith, 1992, Success Publications.

Antiques, buying and selling: *How to Make a Living in Antiques*, William Ketchum, 1990, Henry Holt; *How to Buy and Sell Antiques at a Profit*, Dan Shiaras, 1991, Shiaras Antiques; *How to be Successful in the Antique Business: A Survival Handbook*, Ronald Barlow, 1980, Windmill Publishing.

Antiques, restoring: *How to Restore Antiques*, Larry Freeman, 1960, American Life Foundation.

Apartment preparation service: *How to Start and Manage an Apartment Preparation Service Business*, Jerre Lewis and Lewlie Renn, 1996, Lewis Renn.

Appliance repair: *How to Make a Fortune in Appliance Repair*, Staff, 1992, Gordon Press; *How to Start and Operate Your Own Major Appliance Repair Business*, Rey Longhurst, 1988, R. Longhurst.

Appraiser, real estate: Contact the American Institute of Real Estate Appraisers, 430 North Michigan Avenue, Chicago, IL, 60611, 312-329-8559; *Appraising Residences and Income Properties*, Henry Harrison, 1992, H Squared Company.

Aquarium maintenance in homes, offices, or other commercial sites: *Aquarium Maintenance Guide: Freshwater*, Larry McGee, 1996, Aquarium Attract; *Aquarium Fish*, Staff, 1996, DK Publishing.

Architect: *Architect in Practice*, David Chappell and Christopher Willis, 1992, Blackwell Science.

Art, creating and selling: *The Business of Being an Artist*, Daniel Grant, 1991, Allworth Press; *How to Survive and Prosper as an Artist*, Caroll Michels, 1992, Henry Holt; *This Business of Art*, Diane Cochrane, 1988, Watson-Guptill.

Astrologer: *How to be a Great Astrologer: The Planetary Aspects Explained*, James Braha, 1992, Hermetician Press.

Audio-visual repair services: *Troubleshooting and Repairing Audio and Video Cassette Players and Recorders*, Homer Davidson, 1992, TAB Books.

Auditing utility bills: *How to Make Easy Money Auditing Home Utility Bills: A New, Simple Guide to Refunds and Reductions*, Larry Etherington, 1992, UAS Publishing.

Automobile dealer, new or used: *Used Car Sales*, Guide Number N2330, Entrepreneur.

Automobile detailing: *Auto Detailing Service: Over $100,000 a Year In Auto Detailing*, Guide Number N1146, Entrepreneur.

Automobile mechanic: *Find a Career in Auto Mechanics*, C. William Harrison, Putnam; *Troubleshooting and Repairing Cars*, Homer Davidson, 1990, TAB Books.

Automotive refinishing: *Complete Guide to Automotive Refinishing*, Harry Chudy, 1987, Prentice-Hall.

Automobile upholstery repair: *How to Restore Auto Upholstery*, John Lee, 1994, Motorbooks International.

Automobile, truck, or trailer rental: *Used Car Rental Agency*, Guide Number N1108, Entrepreneur.

Baby sitting: *How to Make More Money Babysitting*, Richard O'Keef, 1992, Diamond Books; *How To Be a Super Sitter*, Lee Salk and Jay Litvin, 1990, NTC Publishing Group.

Baking, for restaurants, special occasions and wedding cakes: *Cooking for Profit: the Business of Food Preparation* (trade magazine), P.O.Box 267, Fond du Lac, WI, 54935; *Baking Home Market*, Staff, 1995, Rector Press.

Balloon designs and bouquets: *How to Become a Balloon Artist and Make Up to One Hundred Thousand Dollars a Year*, Charles Prosper, 1987, Global Publishing.

Basket making: *Start a Craft: Basket Making*, Polly Pollock, 1994, Book Sales.

Bath and kitchen remodeling: *Kitchen Remodeling*, Guide Number N1105, Entrepreneur.

Beautician: *Successful Salon Management*, E.J.Tezak, 1985, Milady Publishers; *How You Can Make Money in the Hairdressing Business*, R. W. Jeremiah, 1982, S. Thornes; *Start and Run a Profitable Beauty Salon: A Complete Step-by-Step Business Plan*, Paul Pogue, TAB Books.

Bed and breakfast inn proprietor: *How to Start and Run Your Own Bed and Breakfast Inn*, Ripley Hotch and Carl Glassman, 1992, Stackpole; *How to Open and Operate a Bed and Breakfast*, Jan Stankus, 1992, Globe Pequot; *Start and Run a Profitable Bed and Breakfast*, Monica Taylor, 1992, Self-Counsel Press.

Beekeeping and honey sales: *ABC and XYZ of Bee Culture: An Encyclopedia of Beekeeping*, Roger Morse and Kim Flottum, 1990, A.I.Root.

Bodywork (automobiles): *How to Repair and Restore Bodywork*, David Hacobs, 1991, Motorbooks International.

Bookkeeping and tax preparation: *Start and Build a Prosperous Bookkeeping, Tax and Financial Service Business*, Gordon Lewis, 1996, Acton Circle.

Books, buying and selling used: *How to Buy and Sell Old Books*, L. Freeman, 1965, American Life Foundation; *Start and Run a Profitable Secondhand Bookstore*, Tracey Jone, 1996, Self-Counsel Press; *How to Start and Manage a Used Bookstore Business*, Jerre Lewis and Leslie Renn, 1996, Lewis Renn.

Bookbinding service: *Simplified Bookbinding*, Henry Gross, 1976, Scribner.

Bookkeeping service: *Bookkeeping on Your Home-Based PC*, Lisa Stern, 1993, TAB Books; *Bookkeeping Service*, Guide Number N2335, Entrepreneur.

Book producer: Contact the American Book Producers Association, Fourth Floor, 319 East 52nd Street, New York, NY, 10022, 212-982-8934.

Brewery operator: *How to Open a Brew Pub or Microbrewery*, Bruce Winner and Scott Smith, 1995, American Brewers.

Builder: *How to Become a Builder: Without Capital or Experience*, Harold R. Muxlow, 1988, TGH Publishing.

Butchering and sausage making: *Home Butchering and Meat Preservation*, Geeta Dordick, 1986, TAB Books.

Cake decorating: *How to Make Money in Cake Decorating*, Del Carnes, 1987, Deco-Press Publishers.

Calligrapher: *How to Become a Professional Calligrapher*, Stuart David, 1985, Taplinger.

Candles, making and selling: *How to Make Candles and Money*, Charles Koch, 1964, Borden.

Carpentry: *Opportunities in Carpentry Careers*, Roger Sheldon, 1987, VGM Horizons; *How to Open and Operate a Home-Based Carpentry Business*, Charlie Self, 1995, Globe Pequot.

Carpets, floors, and drapes; cleaning and installation: *How to Sell and Price Contract Cleaning*, William Griffin, 1988, Cleaning Consultants; *Carpet Cleaning Service*, Guide Number N1053, Entrepreneur; *How to Start and Manage a Carpet-Cleaning Service Business: Step by Step Guide to Business Success*, Jerre Lewis and Leslie Renn, 1996, Lewis Renn.

Cartoon drawing and selling: *How to Draw and Sell Cartoons*, Ross Thompson and Bill Hewison, 1985, North Light Books.

Catering service (weddings, parties and picnics): *How to Open and Operate a Home-Based Catering Business*, Denise Vivaldo, 1993, Globe Pequot; *Start and Run a Profitable Catering Business: From Thyme and Timing*, George Erdosh, 1994, Self-Counsel Press; *How to Beome a Caterer: Everything You Need to Know from Finding Clients to the Final Bill*, Susan Wright, 1996, Carol Publishing Group.

Ceramic services, including teaching and selling supplies and equipment: *How to Make Money in Your Ceramic Business*, Dale Swant, 1993, Scott Publishing; *How to Teach Hobby Ceramics*, Judy Ruele, 1989, Scott Publishing MI.

Cheese, making and selling: *The Art of Home Cheesemaking*, Anne Nilsson, 1979, Woodbridge Press.

Child care: *Start Your Own At-Home Child Care Business*, Patricia Gallagher, 1994, Doubleday; *Family Day Care: How to Provide It in Your Home*, Betsy Squibb, 1986, Harvard Common Press; *Start Your Own Latchkey Program*, Miriam Charnow, 1989, National Council on Aging; *Starting and Operating a Child Care Center: A Guide*, Lillie Robinson, 1994, Readers Press.

Child care referral service: *How to Run a Profitable Child-Care Referral Service*, William Frederick, 1994, International Wealth.

Children's parties promoter: *How to Give Children's Parties*, Gilly Cubitt and Judy Williams, 1992, Smithmark.

Chimney sweep and stove cleaning: *Chimneys and Stove Cleaning*, Staff, GardenWay Publishing.

Christmas trees, growing and selling: *How to Grow and Sell Christmas Trees*, 1988, Outdoor Publishing.

Cleaning service: *How to Start Your Own Cleaning Business with as Little as Five Dollars: A Step by Step Guide for the Housecleaning Business*, Vikki Wachuku-Stokes, 1990, Vikkis Creative; *Cleaning Up for a Living*, Don Aslett and Mark Browning, 1991, Betterway; *Start and Run a Profitable Home Cleaning Business*, Susan Bewsey, 1995, Self-Counsel Press.

Clipping service: *Starting and Operating a Clipping Service*, Demaris Smith, 1987, Pilot Books.

Closet organizer: *Closet Customizing*, Guide Number N1291, Entrepreneur.

Clothing recycling: *Clothing Recycling as a Home or Small Business*, Data Notes Publishing Staff, 1992, Prosperity and Profits.

Coin dealer: *How to Be a Successful Coin Dealer*, David Bowers, 1988, Bowers and Merena.

Collection agency: *Collection Agency*, Guide Number N1207, Entrepreneur.

Commercial photographer: *Photo Business Careers*, Art Evans, 1990, Photo Data Research.

Commercial producer for television or radio: *How to Produce Effective TV Commercials*, Hooper White, 1994, NTC Publishing Group.

Communications business: *How to Open and Operate a Home-Based Communications Business*, Louann Werksma, 1995, Globe Pequot.

Computer businesses: *Making Money With Your Computer at Home*, Paul Edwards and Sarah Edwards, 1993, Tarcher; *Home Office Computer Book*, Steve Rimmer, 1991, Sybex; *How to Make a Fortune with Your Computer*, Jan Jablonski, 1993, Lion Publishing; *How to Build a Successful Business with a Computer*, 1991, Gordon Press; *Making Money on the Internet*, Alfred Glossbrenner, 1995, TAB Books; *How to Be a Successful Computer Consultant*, Alan Simon, 1990, McGraw; *Computer Consultant's Guide: Real-Life Strategies for Building a Successful Consulting Career*, Janet Ruhl, 1994, Wiley; *Computer Consulting on Your Home-Based PC*, Herman Holtz, 1994, McGraw; *Make Money with Your PC! A Guide to Starting and Running a Successful Computer-Based Business*, Lynn Waldorf, 1994, Ten Speed Press; *Office '97: The Complete Reference*, Stephen Nelson and Peter Weverka, 1997, Berkeley; *Word Processing Profits at Home*, Peggy Glenn, 1993, Aames-Allen. Also see the monthly, *Home Office Computing*, available on news-stands. You might also subscribe to moonlight-1. This is designed for anyone interested in moonlighting from home with their computer. To subscribe, send a message to the following e-mail address: mortz@netcome.com with the text "subscribe moonlight-1 Your Real Name."

Computer service and maintenance: *Service News*, Box 995, Yarmouth ME 04096 (periodical); *Start Your Own Computer Repair Business*, Linda Rohrbough, 1995, McGraw; *Troubleshooting and Repairing Computer Monitors*, Stephen Bigelow, 1995, TAB Books.

Construction work: *How to Succeed with Your Own Construction Business*, Stephen Diller, 1990, Craftsman.

Construction cleanup: *Construction Cleanup*, Guide Number N2328, Entrepreneur.

Consultant: *How to Become a Successful Consultant in Your Own Field*, Hubert Bermont, 1991, Prima Publications; *How to Start and Operate Your Own Profitable Consulting Business*, Irwin Nathason, 1990, Worldwide Marketing; *How to Be a Consultant*, Sally Garratt, 1991, Ashgate Publishing; *How to Make It Big as a Consultant*, William Cohen, 1993, AMACOM; *Start and Run a Profitable Consulting Business*, Douglas Gray, 1995, Self-Counsel Press.

Cook and cooking classes: *How to Become Profitably Self-Employed in Your Own Creative Cooking Business*, Janet Shown, 1983, Live Oak Publishers.

Copy shop: *How to Start and Manage an Instant Print/Copy Shop Business*, Jerre Lewis and Lewlis Renn, 1996, Lewis Renn.

Cosmetology: *How to Start and Manage a Cosmetology Business*, Jerre Lewis and Leslie Renn, 1995, Lewis Renn.

Craft school: *Starting a Home Sewing-Craft School*, Allan Smith, 1994, Success Publishing.

Crafts, making, and selling: *Start and Run a Profitable Craft Business: A Step-by-Step Plan*, William Hynes, 1993, Self-Counsel Press; *Selling to Catalog Houses*, 1987, and *How to Sell Your Homemade Creations*, Allan Smith, 1992, both from Success Publications; *Crafts Marketing Success Secrets*, Barbara Brabec, 1988, Brabec Productions; *How to be a Weekend Entrepreneur: Making Money at Craft Fairs, Trade Shows and Swap Meets*, Susan Ratliff, 1991, Marketing Methods Press; *Creative Cash: How to Sell Your Crafts, Needlework, Designs and Know-how*, Barbara Brabec, 1991, Brabec Productions; *How to Start Making Money with Your Crafts*, Kathryn Caputo, 1995, Betterway.

Dance instructor; ballet, jazz and tap or social and ballroom: *How to Operate a Successful Dance Studio*, C. Farrell, 1986, Gordon Press.

Day-care center operator: *Family Day Care: How to Provide It in Your Own Home*, Betsy Squibb, 1986, Harvard Common Press.

Deli shop: *How to Start and Manage a Sandwich Shop/Deli Business*, Jerre Lewis and Lewlie Renn, 1995, Lewis Renn.

Delivery service: *How to Earn $15 to $50 an Hour With a Pickup or Van*, Don Lilly, 1987, Darian Books.

Desktop publishing: *How to Start Your Own Desktop Publishing Business*, Robert Brenner and Scott Olson, 1992, Brenner Information Group; *Start Your Own*

Desktop Publishing Business, Pfeiffer Staff, 1994, Pfeiffer and Company; *How to Make Money Publishing City and Regional Magazines*, Thomas Williams, 1994, Venture Press.

Dietician: *Opportunities in Nutrition Careers*, Carol Caldwell, 1986, VGM Career Horizons.

Dolls, repair and restore: *How to Repair and Restore Dolls*, Barbara Koval, 1994, Seven Hills Books.

Earthworm farming: *How to Raise Earthworms for Profit*, Jack Frost, 1991, Longhurst.

Editing: *How to Start and Run a Writing and Editing Business*, Herman Holtz, 1992, Wiley.

Elder care: *Senior Day Care*, Guide Number N1335, Entrepreneur; *How to Start and Manage a Nursing Home Care Business*, Jerre Lewis and Leslie Renn, 1996, Lewis Renn.

Electrician: *Exploring Careers as An Electrician*, Marilyn Jones, 1987, Rosen Publishing.

Electroplating: *How to Start and Operate an Electroplating Shop*, Randell Nyborg, 1988, Universal Publishing House.

Employment agency: *Employment Agency*, Guide Number N1051, Entrepreneur.

Estate practice: *How to Build a Successful Estate Practice*, Robert Hunter, 1984, Clark Boardman Callaghan.

Event planner and promoter: *Event Planning Service*, Guide Number N1313, Entrepreneur.

Farming: *How to Make Money in Small-Scale Farming*, 1991, Gordon Press.

Farm machinery repair: *How to Start and Manage a Farm Equipment Repair Service Business*, Jerre Lewis and Leslie Renn, 1995, Lewis Renn.

Fashion designer: *How to Become a Fashion Designer*, Jill Miller-Lewis, 1987, Miller Designs.

Fish farmer: *How to Start and Manage a Fish Farming Business*, Jerre Lewis and Leslie Renn, 1995, Lewis Renn.

Flea market sales: *How to Make Money in Flea Markets*, Roger Williams, 1993, Rogers Spec.

Food specialties (baked goods, candy, herbs and spices, pastas, preserves, spiced vinegars): *From Kitchen to Market: Selling Your Gourmet Food Specialty*, Stephen Hall, 1996, Upstart Publishing.

Furnace installation and maintenance: *Getting Started in Heating and Air Conditioning Service*, Allen Russell, 1976, Business News Publishing.

Garage sales: *How to Have High Dollar Garage Sales: Complete Guide to an Easy More Profitable Sale*, Jean Hines, 1989, Vista Mark; *Backyard Money Machine: How to Organize and Operate a Successful Garage Sale*, I.R. Schmelz, 1995, Silver Streak.

Gift basket service: *How to Find Your Treasure in a Gift Basket*, R. Perkins, 1991, R. Perkins; *Start Your Own Gift Basket Business*, JoAnn Padgett, 1993, Business Concepts; *Start and Run a Profitable Gift Basket Business*, Mardi Foster-Walker, 1995, Self-Counsel Press.

Guard service: *How to Start and Manage a Guard Service Business*, Leslie Renn and Jerre Lewis, 1995, Lewis Renn.

Graphic design and illustration: *Running a Successful Graphic Design Business*, Nat Bakar, 1991, Art Direction.

Greenhouse operation: *Greenhouse and Nursery Handbook: A Complete Guide to Growing and Selling Ornamental Container Plants*, Francis Jozwik, 1992, Andmar Press.

Guns, buying and selling: *How to Buy and Sell Used Guns*, John Traister, 1982, Stoeger Publishing.

Heating and air conditioning service: *Starting in Heating and Air Conditioning Service*, L.E. LaRocque, 1992, Business News.

Health care occupations including home nursing, dentistry, optometry, physical therapy and a myriad of other types of health care: *How to Start and Manage a Home Health Care Business*, Jerri Lewis and Leslie Renn, 1996, Lewis Renn.

Health care services: *Health Service Businesses on Your Home-Based PC*, Rick Benzel, 1993, TAB Books.

Herb gardening, selling herbs, potpourri: *Herbal Treasures for Gardening, Cooking and Crafts*, Phyllis Shaudys, 1990, Storey Communications; *Making and Selling Herbal Crafts*, Alyce Nadeau, 1995, Sterling.

Home inspection for prospective buyers, banks: *Home Inspection Service*, Guide Number N1334, Entrepreneur.

House cleaning: *How to Start and Manage a Housecleaning Service Business*, Jerre Lewis and Leslie Renn, 1996, Lewis Renn.

House painting: *House Painting*, Guide Number N1249, Entrepreneur.

House sitting: *How to Design-Own-and Operate a Successful Homesitter Service*, Maxine Sommers, 1996, Pound Sterling.

Illustrator: *How to Be a Successful Illustrator: A Practical Guide*, Ray Evans, 1994, Batsford UK Trafalgar.

Image consultant: *Fashion News and Views*, publication of the Association of Fashion and Image Consultants, 7655 Old Springhouse Road, Suite 211, McLean, VA, 703- 848-2664.

Importing and exporting: *Importing: A Practical Guide to an Exciting and Rewarding Business*, Anne Curran and Glen Mullett, 1992, ISC Press; *Importing As a Small Business*, John Spiers, 1988, Five Star; *Export-Import: Everything You and Your Company Need to Know to Compete in World Markets*, Joseph A. Zodl, 1992, Betterway; *How to Make a Fortune Through Export Mail Order Riches*, Tyler Hicks, 1992, Lion Publishing; *How to Export: Everything You Need to Know to Get Started*, Roger Fritz, 1991, Probus Publishing; *How to be an Importer and Pay for Your World Travel*, Mary Green and Stanley Gillmar, 1992, Ten Speed Press.

Income tax preparation service: *Tax Preparation Service*, Guide Number N2332, Entrepreneur.

Information broker: *How You Can Make a Fortune Selling Information by Mail*, Russ Von Hoelscher, 1991, Profit Ideas; *The Information Broker's Handbook*, Sue Rugge, 1992, McGraw; *Information for Sale: How to Start and Operate Your Own Data Research Service*, John Everett, 1994, TAB Books.

Interior decorator: *Interior Design Business Handbook: A Complete Guide to Profitability*, Mary Knackstedt and Laura Haney, 1992, Van Nostrand Reinhold; *Start Your Own Interior Design Business*, Linda Ramsay, 1994, Touch Design; *How to Make More Money at Interior Design*, Robert Alderman, 1982, Interior Design.

Inventor: *How to be a Successful Inventor: Turn your Ideas into Profit*, Gordon Griffin, 1991, Wiley; *How to Get Rich with Your Idea or Invention: A Complete Step-by-Step Manual*, Roger Hooper, 1989, Hooper Group; *How to Sell and Promote Your Idea, Project, or Invention*, Reece Franklin, 1993, Prima.

Investor: *How to Be a Successful Investor*, Bailard, Hiehl and Kaiser, Inc. Staff, 1989, Irwin Professional Publishing

Janitorial services: *Janitorial Service*, Guide Number N1034, Entrepreneur.

Jewelry fabrication and repair: *Jewelry Manufacture and Repair*, Charles Jarvis, 1990, Antique Collectors; *How to Be Successful in the Bead Jewelry Business*, Kate Drew-Williams, 1994, Nomad Press International.

Landlord: *How to Be a Landlord: A Primer for First-Time Landlords*, Mary and Gary Tondorf-Dick, 1985, Doubleday; *Landlord's Handbook: A Complete Guide to Managing Small Residential Properties*, Daniel Goodwin and Richard Reesdorf, 1988, Dearborn Financial Publishing.

Landscaping: *How to Open and Operate a Home-Based Landscaping Business*, Owen Dell, 1994, Globe Pequot.

Language translation service: *Language Translation Services*, Guide Number N1353, Entrepreneur.

Lawn care: *Lawn Aeration: Turn Hard Soil into Cold Cash*, Robin Pedroti, 1992, Prego Press; *Lawn Care and Gardening: a Down-to-Earth Guide to the Business*, Kevin Rossi, 1994, Acton Circle; *Starting and Operating a Landscape Maintenance Business*, Lawrence Price, 1989, Botany Books.

Lawn mower sharpening and repair: *How to Sharpen Every Blade in Your Workshop*, Don Geary, 1994, Betterway.

Lawyer and legal services: *Legal Services on Your Home-Based PC*, Rick Benzel, 1994, TAB Books; *How to Start and Build a Law Practice*, Jay Foonberg, 1991, American Bar Association.

Limousine service: *How to Start and Operate a Limousine Service*, Randell Nyborg, 1990, Universal Publishing House.

Literary agency: *How to Be a Literary Agent: An Introductory Guide to Literary Representation*, Richard Mariotti, 1995, Piccadilly Books.

Livestock breeding: *Applied Animal Reproduction*, Joe Bearden, 1980, Reston Publishing.

Locksmithing: *Locksmithing*, F.A. Steel, 1982, TAB Books.

Logging and timber cutting: *Timber Cutting Practices*, Steve Conway, 1978, Miller Freeman Publications.

Maid service: *Maid Service*, Guide Number N1343, Entrepreneur; *How to Start Your Own Maid Service*, Sondra Koenig, 1994, Maid Service.

Mail drop service: *Private Postal Boxes, Mail Addresses and Mail Forwarding Services: A How to Find or Locate Workbook*, Frieda Carrol, 1983, Prosperity and Profits; *How to Use Mail Drops for Privacy and Profit*, Jack Luger, 1988, Loompanics.

Mailing lists preparation: *How to Compile and Sell Mailing Lists*, 1991, Gordon Press; *How to Use, Compile, Maintain and Sell Mailing Lists*, Neal Michaels, 1992, Premier Publishers.

Mail order: *How to Start and Operate a Mail Order Business*, Julian Simon, 1993, Bell Springs Publishing; *Start and Run a Profitable Mail-Order Business: Getting Started for under $500: Your Step-by-Step Business Plan*, Robert Blym, 1996, Self-Counsel Press; *Sell Anything by Mail*, Frank Jefkins, 1990, Adams; *How to Build a Multi-Million Dollar Catalog Mail Order Business by Someone Who Did*, Lawson Hill, 1984, Prentice Hall; *How to Make a Fortune in Your Own Drop-Ship Mail Order Business*, Duane Shinn, 1990, Shinn; *Home-Based Mail Order: A Success Guide for Entrepreneurs*, William Bond, 1990, McGraw.

Maintenance and repair service: *How to Become a Maintenance and Repair Handy-Person and Have Real Job Security*, Robert Stuart, 1992, Pro-Guides.

Manicurist: *West's Textbook of Manicures*, Jerry Ahern, 1986, West Publishing; *Nail Salon*, Guide Number N1274, Entrepreneur.

Manufacturing: *Manufacturing Strategy: How to Formulate and Implement a Winning Plan*, John Miltenburg, 1995, Productivity Press; *Manufacturing Beyond Joe's Garage: Value Based Manufacturing*, William Miller, 1995, Bayrock.

Martial arts school: *Martial Artist Business Kit*, Keven Hampton, 1993, High Desert Press.

Masseur/masseuse: *Massage: A Career at Your Fingertips*, Martin Ashley, 1995, Enterprise Publishing.

Medical claims processing: *Medical Claims Processing*, Guide Number N1345, Entrepreneur; *How to Start and Manage a Medical Claims Processing Business*, Jerre Lewis and Leslie Renn, 1996, Lewis Renn.

Medical transcriptionist: *The Independent Medical Transcriptionist*, Avila-Weil, 1994, Rayve Productions.

Metalworking: *Metal Workers Benchtop Reference Manual*, Joseph Serafin, 1986, TAB Books.

Money management service: *How to Start Your Own Money Management Business*, Douglas Harman, 1994, Irwin Professional Publishing.

Monogramming: *Monogram Business Booklet*, free from Meistergram, S.R. Gluskin, 5501 Cass Avenue, Cleveland, OH, 44113.

Music (writing, performing, teaching): *Making Money Making Music*, James Dearing, 1990, and *Songwriter's Market*, annual, both from Writer's Digest Books; *How to Get a Nightclub Gig: A Singer's Guide*, Dolores Del Rae, 1985,

SOS Publishing; *How to Make More in Music: A Freelance Guide*, James Gibson, 1984, Workbooks Press; *Making Money Teaching Music*, Barbara Newsam and David Newsam, 1995, Writer's Digest; *Career Opportunities in the Music Industry*, Sherry Field, 1996, Facts on File; *How to Become a Successful Nashville Songwriter*, Michael Kosser, 1981, Prima Publishing.

Musical instruments, repair: *How to Repair Violins and Other Musical Instruments*, Alfred Common, 1977, Gordon Press.

Newsletter writer, publisher: *Home-based Newsletter Publishing: A Success Guide for Entrepreneurs*, William Bond, 1992, McGraw; *Making Money Writing Newsletters*, Elaine Floyd, 1994, Newsletter Resources; *Start Your Own Desktop Publishing Business*, Pfeiffer Staff, 1994, Pfeiffer.

Notary public: *How to Become a Notary Public*, Daniel Barness, 1987, Duane Books; *Earning Extra Income As a Notary*, *National Notary* Magazine editors, 1993, National Notary.

Nursery operator: *How to Start and Manage a Nursery Business*, Jerre Lewis and Leslie Renn, 1995, Lewis Renn.

Nursing: *Homecare* Magazine, 2048 Cotner Avenue, Los Angeles, CA, 90025, (periodical) 213-477-1033.

Nursing home operator: *Running Your Own Private Residential or Nursing Home*, Colin Barron, 1990, Taylor and Francis.

Packaging and shipping service: *Packaging and Shipping Service*, Guide Number N1287, Entrepreneur.

Painting, house exterior, and interior: *Painting Contractor: Start and Run a Money-Making Business*, Don Ramsey, 1994, TAB Books.

Paperhanging service: *How to Become a Financially Successful Paperhanging Entrepreneur*, Stanley Warshaw, 1981, U.S. School Professionals; *Wallpapering*, Outlet Staff, 1994, Random House Value.

Paralegal: *The Independent Paralegal's Handbook*, Ralph Warner, 1994, Nolo Press; *Starting and Managing Your Own Business: A Freelancing Guide for Paralegals*, Dorothy Secol, 2994, Wiley.

Party planner, children's, and adult: *Event Planning Service: People Will Pay You To Plan Their Parties*, Guide Number N1313, Entrepreneur.

Personnel referral and personnel services: *How to Start and Manage a Personnel Referral Service Business*, Jerre Lewis and Leslie Renn, 1995, Lewis

Renn; *Profitable Personnel Services: Start and Run a Money-Making Business*, Kristi Mishel, 1995, TAB Books.

Pest control service: *Pest Control*, Guide Number N1280, Entrepreneur; *How to Start and Manage a Pest Control Service Business*, Jerri Lewis and Leslie Renn, 1995, Lewis Renn.

Pet boarding, sitting, walking: *Pet Sitting for Profit*, Patti Moran, 1987, New Beginnings.

Pet grooming, training: *Pet Hotel and Grooming Service*, Guide Number N1033, Entrepreneur.

Pet photography: *Profitable Pet Photography*, Embee Staff, 1988, Embee Press.

Photography; weddings, special events, portraits, passport photos: *How to Start and Run a Successful Photography Business*, Gerry Kopelow, 1992, Images; *The Professional Photographer: Developing a Successful Career*, Larry Goldman, 1983, Doubleday; *Careers in Photography*, Art Evans, 1992, Photo Data Research; *How to Open and Operate a Home-Based Photography Business*, Kenn Oberrecht, 1993, Globe Pequot; *How to Sell Your Photos to a Stock Agency*, Embee Staff, 1988, Embee Press.

Physical therapist: *Physical Therapy*, Bernice Krumhansl, 1989, NTC Publishing Group; *How to Become a Physical Therapist*, Skip Hunter and Lori Whitlow, 1996, S. Hunter.

Piano lessons: *How to Teach Piano Successfully*, James Bastien, 1989, Kjos.

Piano tuning: *Piano Tuning: A Simple and Accurate Method for Amateurs*, J. Fischer, 1976, Dover.

Picture framing service: *Picture Framing: A Practical Guide to All Aspects of the Art and the Craft*, Pete Bingham, 1993, Stackpole.

Plant maintenance in offices and homes: *Plant Care*, Staff of Best of Fine Gardening Service, 1994, Taunton.

Plant grower, gardener, truck farmer: *How to Make Money Growing Plants, Trees and Flowers*, Francis Jozwik, 1992, Andmar Press; *Backyard Cash Crops*, Craig Wallin, 1989, Homestead Design.

Plumbing: *Plumbing Contractor: Start and Run a Money-Making Business*, Dodge Woodson, 1993, McGraw.

Pool maintenance: *Pool Cleaning and Repair*, Guide Number N1285, Entrepreneur.

Potter, making and selling pottery: *Studio Pottery*, Oliver Watson, 1993, Chronicle Books.

Printer and quick printing services: *How to Start and Manage a Printing Business*, Jerre Lewis and Leslie Renn, 1995, Lewis Renn.

Printing T-shirts: *How to Print T-Shirts for Fun and Profit*, Scott Fresener, 1994, Union Ink.

Private detective or investigator: *How to Make $100,000 a Year as a Private Investigator*, Edmund Pankau, 1993, Paladin Press.

Process server (delivers legal documents): *How to Make Money as a Process Server*, Ralph Thomas, 1986, Thomas Publishing.

Professional services (doctor, lawyer, nursing): *Private Practice Handbook: The Tools, Tactics and Techniques for Successful Practice Development*, Charles Browning, 1982, Duncliffs International.

Psychological testing and counseling: *Psychological Testing and Assessment Instructor's Manual*, Mark Swerdlik, 1995, Mayfield Publishing.

Public relations agent: Contact The Public Relations Society of America Incorporated, 33 Irving Place, New York, NY, 10003, 212-861-0630; *Starting a Public Relations Firm*, Ruth Smith, 1988, Business Of Your Own.

Public speaking: *How to Make a Fortune from Public Speaking*, Robert Anthony, 1988, Berkley.

Publishing: *How to be Your Own Publisher, Advertiser, Promoter*, Staff, 1993, Prosperity and Profits; *You Publish It: How to Start a Home Publishing Company for Under One Hundred Dollars*, Robert Cooper, 1994, Cooper House.

Quilting, knitting, weaving: *Quiltmaking Tips and Techniques: Over 1,000 Creative Ideas to Make Your Quiltmaking Quicker, Easier and Lots More Fun*, Jane Townswick, 1994, Rodale Press.

Reading service: *Make Money Reading Books: How to Start and Operate Your Own Home-Based Freelance Reading Service*, Bruce Fife, 1993, Piccadilly Books; *Earn Money Reading Books*, Robert Hancock, 1988, Broughton Hall.

Real estate: *Real Estate Agent*, Jack Rudman, 1991, National Learning; *How to Make Big Money in Real Estate in the Tighter '90s Market*, Tyler Hicks, 1992, Prentice Hall; *How to Build a Real Estate Money Machine*, Wade Cook, 1990, Focus; *How to Build Your Real-Estate Fortune on Other People's Money*, Tyler Hicks, 1992, International Wealth; *Up and Running in 30 Days: Make Money Your First Month in Real Estate*, Carla Cross, 1995, Dearborn Financial Publishing.

Refuse removal and recycling service: *Refuse Recycling and Recovery*, John Holmes, 1981, Books Demand; *How to Start and Operate a Recycling Business*, John Allison, 1991, RMC Publishing Group.

Remodeling service: *Running Your Remodeling Business*, Harry Hardenbrook, 1988, Craftsman.

Renovate, resell real estate: *Profits in Buying and Renovating Homes*, Lawrence Dworkin, 1990, Craftsman; *How to Make Big Profits Renovating Real Estate*, Robert Gaitens, 1982, Prentice-Hall; *How to Find, Fix and Sell Homes for Profit*, Richard Tollesrud, 1986, Beardsley Press.

Rent inspector: *Rent Inspector*, Jack Rudman, 1994, National Learning Corporation.

Rental property manager: *How to Become an Apartment Manager and Live Rent Free*, Robert Stuart, 1991, Pro-Guides; *Rental Management Made Easy*, W. G. Roberts, 1992, Tower Publishing GA.

Resale shop operator: *How to Open an Elegant Resale Boutique*, Denise Richards, 1977, Pavillion.

Resume writing service: *The Resume Pro*, Yana Parker, 1993, Ten Speed Press; *Start Your Own Resume Writing Business*, Pfeiffer Staff, 1994, Pfeiffer.

Roadside sales: *Profitable Roadside Retailing: Making It Happen*, Gerald Lewis, 1986, Petro Marketing Education Foundation.

Roofing: See *Roofer* Magazine, 12120 Amedicus Lane, Fort Myers, FL, 33907, 813-275-763; *Complete Roofing Handbook*, James Brumbaugh, 1986, Collier Macmillan.

Rubber stamps, made to order: *How to Build Your Own Rubber Stamp Press*, 1978, Billy Mason, Kelso.

Sales representative: *How to Earn Top Dollars As a Manufacturer's Agent*, 1987, Gordon Press; *Making $70,000 a Year As a Self-Employed Manufacturer's Representative*, Leigh Silliphant, 1988, Ten Speed Press.

School operator: *Start Your Own Private School*, Dorie Erickson, 1980, Scandia.

Screen and storm window service, cleaning, repair and installing: *How to Start a Window Cleaning Business*, Judy Suval, 1988, I Can See.

Seamstress, dress design and custom sewing: *Sewing for Profit*, Judith and Allan Smith, 1991, Success Publications; *Sew to Success! How to Make Money in a Home-Based Sewing Business*, Kathleen Spike, 1995, Palmer-Pletsch.

Secretarial services: *Start and Run a Profitable Office Service Business from Your Home: Secretarial Support, Word Processing, Desktop Publishing: Your Step-by-Step Business Plan*, Louise Hagan, 1995, Self-Counsel Press; *How to Start Your Own Home Typing Business*, Joan Cate, 1984, Calabasas Publishing; *How to Open and Operate a Home-Based Secretarial Services Business*, Jan Melnik, 1994, Globe Pequot; *Starting a Secretarial Service*, Business of Your Own Staff, 1988, Business of Your Own; *Start Your Own Secretarial Service Business*, Pfeiffer Staff, 1994, Pfeiffer.

Security and protection services: *Burglar Alarm Sales/Installation*, Guide Number N1091, Entrepreneur.

Seminar planner and presenter: *How to Make It Big in the Seminar Business*, Paul Darasik, 1992, McGraw.

Sharpening hand tools and scissors: *How to Sharpen Every Blade in Your Workshop*, Don Geary, 1994, Betterway Books.

Shopping services for aged, disabled and those too busy (food, gifts): *A Business For People "Born To Shop"*, Guide Number N1310, Entrepreneur.

Sign fabrication, installation: *Ralph Gregory's Sign Painting Techniques*, Ralph Gregory, 1973, Signs of the Times Publishing.

Small animal breeding: *How to Raise Rabbits for Fun and Profit*, Milton Faive, 1973, Nelson-Hall; Storey Communications publishes many books on raising small animals. For a free catalog write Storey Communications, Schoolhouse Road, Pownal, VT 05261.

Sports training schools and camps operator: *Physical Fitness Center*, Guide Number N1172, Entrepreneur.

Stable operator: *Running a Stable as a Business*, Janet MacDonald, 1990, J.A. Allen.

Stained glass crafting: See *Professional Stained Glass*, Route 6 at Dingle Ridge Road, P.O. Box 69, Brewster, NY, 10509; *Practical Stained Glass Crafting*, Jo Frohbieter-Mueller, 1984, David and Charles.

Stencilling: *Stencilling Techniques: A Complete Guide to Traditional and Contemporary Designs for the Home*, Jane Gauss, 1995, Watson-Gupill.

Tax consultant and tax return preparation: *How You Can Make Money As a Property Tax Consultant*, Lynn Tylczak, 1992, Prentice Hall.

Taxidermy: *How to Make Extra Profits in Taxidermy*, John Phillips, 1984, New Win Publishing.

Teaching and tutoring, including teaching English in immigrant communities, music, use of modern equipment, basic subjects: *The Teaching Marketplace: Make Money With Freelance Teaching, Corporate Training, and on the Lecture Circuit*, Bart Brodsky, 1991, Community Resource Institute; *How to Make Money Teaching Reading at Home*, James Shaw, 1984, Mark Excell Publishing.

Teddy bears, make and sell: *How to Make and Sell Quality Teddy Bears*, Terry Michaud and Doris Michaud, 1986, Hobby House.

Telemarketing: *Telemarketing* Magazine, 17 Park Street, Norwalk, CT, 06851.

Telephone answering service: *Telephone Answering Service*, Guide Number N1148, Entrepreneur; *How to Start and Manage an Answering Service Business*, Jerri Lewis and Leslie Renn, 1995, Lewis Renn.

Telephone 900 numbers: *Money-Making 900 Numbers: How Entrepreneurs Use the Telephone to Sell Information*, Carol Ginsburg, 1995, Aegis.

Temporary help agency: *Start Your Own Temporary Help Agency*, JoAnn Padgett, 1994, Pfeiffer.

Travel services, agent: *Start and Run a Profitable Travel Agency*, Richard Cropp, 1993, Self-Counsel Press; *How to Become a Spare Time Travel Agent*, Stan Volin, 1987, S. Volin; *How To Be a International Tour Director*, Gerald Mitchell, 1992, *How to Design and Package Tours*, Gerald Mitchell, 1993, and *How to Be a Tour Guide*, Gerald Mitchell, 1992, all from G. E. Mitchell; *Career Opportunities in Travel and Tourism*, John Hauks, 1996, Facts on File.

Tree cutting and trimming: *How to Start and Manage a Tree Service Business*, Jerre Lewis and Leslie renn, 1995, Lewis Renn.

Trout farming: *How to Make a Recreational Trout Farm: Trout Ponds for Fun and Profit*, Jack Frost, 1991, Longhurst.

Type setting service: *How to Start, Operate and Enjoy a Successful Typesetting Business*, Tom Buhl, 1981, Homefront Graphics.

Typing service: *How to Start a Profitable Typing Service at Home*, Nicki Montaperto, 1981, Barnes and Noble.

Tutoring: *How to Teach Adults*, Bill Draves, LERN; *How to Teach a Child to Learn*, Anthony Coletta, 1992, Programs Education.

Upholstering: *Upholstery: A Practical Guide*, Desmond Gaston, 1994, HarperCollins UK.

Vehicle body refinishing: *Vehicle Body Refinishing*, Alan Robinson, 1995, Betterworth-Heinemann.

Vehicle washing: *Vehicle Washing Compliance Manual,* American Trucking Association Staff and Blymyer Engineers Staff, 1995, American Trucking Association.

Vehicle repair: *Truck and Van Repair Manual,* Chilton Automotives Editorial Staff, 1994, Chilton.

Vending machine sales: Contact the National Automatic Merchandising Association, 20 North Wacker Drive, Chicago, IL 60606, 312-346-0370. Also see, American Automatic Blue Book, same address, for a listing of companies that make and sell vending machines. *Vending Times* (a monthly) 545 8th Avenue, New York, NY, 10018, covers practical aspects of the vending business; *How to Make Big Money in the Candy Vending Machine Business,* Julian Aboulafia, 1992, Vantage.

Veterinary services: *Veterinarian,* Jack Rudman, 1994, National Learning Corporation.

Video producer: *How to be an Independent Video Producer,* Bob Jacobs, 1986, Knowledge Industries; *Starting in Video: Costs and Resources Needed,* Kenneth Acton, 1989, Jay Books.

Videographer services (videotaping, editing): *Make Money With Your Camcorder,* Kevin Campbell, 1995, Amherst Media.

Water conditioning installation, maintenance: Contact the Water Quality Association, 4151 Naperville Road, Lisle, IL, 60532.

Wedding co-ordinator, planner: *Wedding Planner,* Guide Number N1330, Entrepreneur.

Welding service: *Welding: Techniques and Rural Practice,* Peter Cryer and Jim Heather, 1996, Buttterworth-Heinemann; *How to Start and Manage a Welding Business,* Jerre Lewis and Leslie Renn, 1994, Lewis Renn.

Well drilling: *Well Drilling Manual,* Scientific Publishers Staff, 1986, Scientific UK.

Wheelchair transportation: *How to Start and Manage a Wheelchair Transportation Business,* Jerre Lewis and Leslie Renn, 1996, Lewis Renn.

Wholesaling and distribution: *Selling on the Fast Track,* Kathy Aaronson, 1989, Putnam.

Window washing: *Window Washer: At Work Above the Clouds,* Keith Greenberg, 1995, Blackbirch.

Window treatments: *Window Treatments*, Karla Nielson, 1989, Van Nos Reinhold.

Wood cutting and delivery for home heating: *How to Start and Manage a Firewood Sales Business*, Jerre Lewis and Leslie Renn, 1996, Lewis Renn.

Woodcrafting and custom furniture: *Make Money from Woodturning*, Ann Phillips, 1995, Sterling; *Making and Repairing Furniture: A Visual Guide*, Klaus Pracht, 1994, Trafalgar.

Workshop, seminar presenter or organizer: *Money Talks: The Complete Guide to Creating a Profitable Workshop or Seminar in Any Field*, Jeffrey Lant, 1995, JLA Publishing.

Word puzzles, writing: *Earn Cash Creating Word Puzzles*, Jacqueline Mallis, 1993, Multi Media.

Writing, freelance: *Writing: Getting Into Print*, Jo Frohbieter-Mueller, 1994, Printed Tree; *Writer's Market*, Staff, annual, Writer's Digest Books; *How to Make Money Writing Corporate Communications*, Mary Collins, 1995, Berkley; *Start and Run a Profitable Freelance Writing Business*, Cristine Adamee, 1994, Self-Counsel Press.

Yoga instructor for classes or individuals: *Yogacise: The No-Sweat Exercise Programme for the '90s*, Lyn Marshall, 1995, Parkwest Publishing.

Other Occupations that May Work for Moonlighters

appraising coins, antiques, and jewelry

auctioneer

automobile painting

automobile, truck, or RV transport service

balloon rides proprietor

barber shop services

bicycle rentals and repair

boat and canoe rental

builders' clean-up service

camp and RV grounds proprietor

camping equipment rental

cards and stationery designing and production

chair caning

chauffeuring

chiropractor

clock and watch repair

companion for shut-ins

concrete work

dating service

drapery fabrication

driving instructor

laundry and ironing service

escort service

excavating

fence installation

floor sanding and cleaning

operating a food wagon for special events

foreign language tutoring

fund-raising for organizations

handbill distribution

hauling service

hayride and sleigh ride operator

holiday decorator

home repairs

home security service

insurance agent

inventory service for businesses

karate instructor

kennel operator

language instruction

preparing and delivering meals to shut-ins

messenger service

modeling school operator

modeling agency

nanny

nanny placement service

newspaper delivery

school bus driver

sealing driveways

sewer cleaning

shoe repair

portable booth snack sales

snow removal

sports instructor

talent agent

taxi service

telephone wake-up service

tilling for gardeners

Resources

Magazines

Many excellent magazines about home businesses are in print. They cover diverse subjects concerning small businesses and include examples of people who have made part-time home businesses work. These publications are a good way to keep current on new laws, new technologies, and old problems. Most of these can be purchased at newsstands. Some of the more useful ones are listed.

Entrepreneur, 2392 Morse Avenue, Irvine, CA, 92714, 800-421-2300.

Home Office Computing, 411 Layfayette, New York, NY, 10003, 212-505-4260.

Income Opportunities, 1500 Broadway, New York, NY, 10036-4015, 212-302-8269.

Spare Time Magazine, 5810 W. Oklahoma Avenue, Milwaukee, WI, 53219, 414-543-8110.

Newsletters

Newsletters are another way to keep apprised of changes in tax law, emerging opportunities, operational tips, and to receive encouragement from other home workers. Your librarian can direct you to newsletters that will fit your specific needs, but a couple of the more general ones are listed below.

Your Successful Home Office, P.O. Box 244, Dillon Beach, CA, 94929. Twelve monthly issues for $24. Excellent articles written by experts in the field of small/home businesses.

BOTTOM LINE/Personal, Boardroom Reports, Inc., 330 West 42nd Street, New York, NY, 10036. Published twice each month, cost $49 per year. Contains valuable, timely information without advertisments.

Most associations print newsletters or tabloids. A couple are listed below. Ask your librarian to help you locate others.

National Association for the Cottage Industry, P.O. Box 14460, Chicago, IL, 60614.

National Association for the Self-Employed, 2316 Gravel Road, Fort Worth, TX, 76118. Membership in this organization includes many financial advantages including group-rate insurance.

The Small Business Administration

The Small Business Administration offers numerous free and inexpensive publications concerning practically every aspect of starting and operating a small business. These publications include practical information and extensive lists of information sources. Call the Small Business Administration Answer Line, 800-827-5722, for a free list of the publications available, or write SBA, P.O. Box 30, Denver, CO, 80201-0030.

Mailing List Houses

Just a few of the hundreds of mailing list houses are included below. They can provide lists of people with very specific interests or characteristics. This is important because the response rate from mailings increases when the recipients are closely targeted or matched with the products or services being advertised. Check the Yellow Pages of your directory for others or ask your local librarian for help.

American List Counsel, 88 Orchard Road, Princeton, NJ, 08540, 908-874-4300, 800-252-5478, Fax 908-874-4433.

Best Mailing Lists, 34 West 32nd Street, New York, NY, 10001, 212-868-1080, 800-692-2378, Fax 212-947-0136.

List Services Corporation, 890 Ethan Allen Highway, Ridgefield, CT, 06877, 201-861-0768.

Qualified Lists Corporation, 135 Bedford Road, Armon, NY, 10504, 914-273-6606.

Computer Online Access Services

Information is at your fingertips from a variety of communication services, but you will discover when you surf the Internet that you can waste hours trying to find useful information. Or, you might subscribe to one service only to discover you need a different one. The editors of *Home Office Computing* magazine selected the following as the most useful online sites. These sites specifically address the many concerns of small business owners and strive to keep them apprised of changes that will affect the way they do business.

CCH Business Owner's Toolkit (Microsoft Network): go word: cch Handy and helpful information from small-business expert CCH on hiring, firing, taxes, and other business essentials.

The Entrepreneur Zone (America Online): keyword: ezone A one-stop source for small business information including information from *Home Office Computing* and other periodicals, plus a regular newsletter, *In The Zone*, that alerts you when new information is added to the site.

Working From Home Forum (CompuServe): go word: work A wealth of software to download, plus solid advice from home-based professionals who know how to market products and build businesses.

Commercial Sites Index (Internet): http://www.directory.net. A complete guide to more than 11,000 commercial home pages on the World Wide Web.

Lycos (Internet): http://lycos.cs.cmu.edu/ Probably the most comprehensive tool for searching the World Wide Web.

Index

From The Oasis Press®
The Leading Publisher of Small Business Information.

At The Oasis Press® we take pride in helping you and two million other businesses grow.

We hope that *Moonlighting* has helped you move closer to a successful business start-up at home, but we also want you to know that The Oasis Press® is your resource for other business issues you may encounter. On the following pages, we offer a brief sampling of The Successful Business Library — books and software that will help you solve your day-to-day business questions as well as prepare you for unexpected problems your business may be facing down the road. We offer up-to-date and practical business solutions, which are easy to use and understand. Call for a complete catalog or let our knowledgeable sales representatives point you in the right direction.

Your input means a lot to us — we hope to hear from you!

Choose from the following related titles to help your business grow.

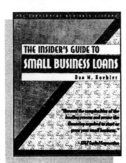

The Insider's Guide to Small Business Loans

Essential for the small business operator in search of capital, this helpful, hands-on guide simplifies the loan application process as never before. The Insider's Guide to Small Business Loans is an easy-to-follow road map designed to help you cut through the red tape and show you how to prepare a successful loan application.

Available in either paperback or binder formats.

Paperback $19.95 (ISBN 1-55571-373-4)
3-Ring Binder $29.95 (ISBN 1-55571-378-5)

New from The Oasis Press®

A complete guide to easily assist you in starting up your own business through today's complex business environment.

SmartStart Your (State) Business

There has never been a better time to start a small business. According to a recent study by the Entrepreneurial Research Consortium, one out of three U.S. households has someone who is involved in a small business startup. With statistics like these, the odds seem to be in your favor... until you start dealing with the many regulations, laws, and financial requirements placed on twenty-first century business owners.

SmartStart Your (State) Business goes a step beyond other business how-to books and provides you with:

- Quick reference to the most current mailing and Internet addresses and telephone numbers for federal, state, local, and private agencies that will help get your business up and running;

- State population statistics, income and consumption rates, major industry trends, and overall business incentives to give you a better picture of doing business in your state.

- Checklists, sample forms, and a complete sample business plan to assist you with the numerous details of start-up.

Also contains advice on forming and registering your business, developing a powerful marketing and public relations plan, guidelines to writing a smart and functional business plan, tips for gaining control of your finances, and advice on company polices.

Available in paperback!

Paperback $19.95 (ISBN varies from state to state, be sure to specify which state you would like.)

The Oasis Press® offers
books and software that will save your time and money!

Updated Edition!

Business Owner's Guide to Accounting & Bookkeeping

Updated and released the fall of 1997! This guide makes understanding the economics of your business simple. Explains the basic accounting principles that relate to any business. Step-by-step instructions for generating accounting statements and interpreting them, spotting errors, and recognizing warning signs. Discusses how creditors view financial statements too.

Available in paperback!
Paperback $19.95 (ISBN 1-55571-381-5)

Top Tax Saving Ideas for Today's Small Business

An extensive summary of every imaginable tax break that is still available in today's "reform" tax environment. The current and helpful resource goes beyond most tax guides on the market that focuses on the tax season only., instead it provides readers with year-round strategies to lower taxes and avoid common pitfalls. Identifies a wide assortment of tax deduction, fringe benefits, and tax deferrals. Includes a simplified checklist of recent tax law changes with an emphasis on tax breaks.

Available in paperback!
Paperback $16.95 (ISBN 1-55571-343-2)

THE OASIS PRESS® ORDER FORM

Call, Mail, Email, or Fax Your Order to: PSI Research, 300 North Valley Drive, Grants Pass, OR 97526 USA
Email: psi2@magick.net   Website: http://www.psi-research.com
Order Phone USA & Canada: +1 800 228-2275   Inquiries & International Orders: +1 541 479-9464 Fax: +1 541 476-1479

TITLE	✔ BINDER	✔ PAPERBACK	QUANTITY	COST
Bottom Line Basics	❏ $39.95	❏ $19.95		
The Business Environmental Handbook	❏ $39.95	❏ $19.95		
Business Owner's Guide to Accounting & Bookkeeping		❏ $19.95		
Buyer's Guide to Business Insurance	❏ $39.95	❏ $19.95		
Collection Techniques for a Small Business	❏ $39.95	❏ $19.95		
A Company Policy and Personnel Workbook	❏ $49.95	❏ $29.95		
Company Relocation Handbook	❏ $39.95	❏ $19.95		
CompControl: The Secrets of Reducing Worker's Compensation Costs	❏ $39.95	❏ $19.95		
Complete Book of Business Forms		❏ $19.95		
Customer Engineering: Cutting Edge Selling Strategies	❏ $39.95	❏ $19.95		
Develop & Market Your Creative Ideas		❏ $15.95		
Doing Business in Russia		❏ $19.95		
Draw The Line: A Sexual Harassment Free Workplace		❏ $17.95		
The Essential Corporation Handbook		❏ $21.95		
The Essential Limited Liability Company Handbook	❏ $39.95	❏ $21.95		
Export Now: A Guide for Small Business	❏ $39.95	❏ $24.95		
Financial Management Techniques for Small Business	❏ $39.95	❏ $19.95		
Financing Your Small Business		❏ $19.95		
Franchise Bible: How to Buy a Franchise or Franchise Your Own Business	❏ $39.95	❏ $24.95		
Friendship Marketing: Growing Your Business by Cultivating Strategic Relationships		❏ $18.95		
Home Business Made Easy		❏ $19.95		
Incorporating Without A Lawyer (Available for 32 states) SPECIFY STATE:		❏ $24.95		
Joysticks, Blinking Lights and Thrills		❏ $18.95		
The Insider's Guide to Small Business Loans	❏ $29.95	❏ $19.95		
InstaCorp – Incorporate In Any State (Book & Software)		❏ $29.95		
Keeping Score: An Inside Look at Sports Marketing		❏ $18.95		
Know Your Market: How to Do Low-Cost Market Research	❏ $39.95	❏ $19.95		
Legal Expense Defense: How to Control Your Business' Legal Costs and Problems	❏ $39.95	❏ $19.95		
Location, Location, Location: How to Select the Best Site for Your Business		❏ $19.95		
Mail Order Legal Guide	❏ $45.00	❏ $29.95		
Managing People: A Practical Guide		❏ $21.95		
Marketing Mastery: Your Seven Step Guide to Success	❏ $39.95	❏ $19.95		
The Money Connection: Where and How to Apply for Business Loans and Venture Capital	❏ $39.95	❏ $24.95		
People Investment	❏ $39.95	❏ $19.95		
Power Marketing for Small Business	❏ $39.95	❏ $19.95		
Profit Power: 101 Pointers to Give Your Business a Competitive Edge		❏ $19.95		
Proposal Development: How to Respond and Win the Bid	❏ $39.95	❏ $21.95		
Raising Capital	❏ $39.95	❏ $19.95		
Retail in Detail: How to Start and Manage a Small Retail Business		❏ $15.95		
Secrets to Buying and Selling a Business		❏ $24.95		
Secure Your Future: Financial Planning at Any Age	❏ $39.95	❏ $19.95		
The Small Business Insider's Guide to Bankers		❏ $18.95		
Start Your Business (Available as a book and disk package – see back)		❏ $ 9.95 (without disk)		
Starting and Operating a Business in...series Includes FEDERAL section PLUS ONE STATE section	❏ $34.95	❏ $27.95		
PLEASE SPECIFY WHICH STATE(S) YOU WANT:				
STATE SECTION ONLY (BINDER NOT INCLUDED) SPECIFY STATE(S):	❏ $8.95			
FEDERAL SECTION ONLY (BINDER NOT INCLUDED)	❏ $12.95			
U.S. EDITION (FEDERAL SECTION – 50 STATES AND WASHINGTON DC IN 11-BINDER SET)	❏ $295.95			
Successful Business Plan: Secrets & Strategies	❏ $49.95	❏ $27.95		
Successful Network Marketing for The 21st Century		❏ $15.95		
Surviving and Prospering in a Business Partnership	❏ $39.95	❏ $19.95		
TargetSmart! Database Marketing for the Small Business		❏ $19.95		
Top Tax Saving Ideas for Today's Small Business		❏ $16.95		
Which Business? Help in Selecting Your New Venture		❏ $18.95		
Write Your Own Business Contracts	❏ $39.95	❏ $24.95		

BOOK SUB-TOTAL (FIGURE YOUR TOTAL AMOUNT ON THE OTHER SIDE)

OASIS SOFTWARE   Please check Macintosh or 3-1/2" Disk for IBM-PC & Compatibles

TITLE	3-1/2" IBM Disk	Mac-OS	Price	QUANTITY	COST
California Corporation Formation Package ASCII Software	☐	☐	$ 39.95		
Company Policy & Personnel Software Text Files	☐	☐	$ 49.95		
Financial Management Techniques (Full Standalone)	☐		$ 99.95		
Financial Templates	☐	☐	$ 69.95		
The Insurance Assistant Software (Full Standalone)	☐		$ 29.95		
Start A Business (Full Standalone)	☐		$ 49.95		
Start Your Business (Software for Windows™)	☐		$ 19.95		
Successful Business Plan (Software for Windows™)	☐		$ 99.95		
Successful Business Plan Templates	☐	☐	$ 69.95		
The Survey Genie - Customer Edition (Full Standalone)	☐		$149.95		
The Survey Genie - Employee Edition (Full Standalone)	☐		$149.95		
SOFTWARE SUB-TOTAL					

BOOK & DISK PACKAGES   Please check whether you use Macintosh or 3-1/2" Disk for IBM-PC & Compatibles

TITLE	IBM-PC	Mac-OS	BINDER	PAPERBACK	QUANTITY	COST
The Buyer's Guide to Business Insurance w/ Insurance Assistant	☐		☐$ 59.95	☐$ 39.95		
California Corporation Formation Binder Book & ASCII Software	☐	☐	☐$ 69.95	☐$ 59.95		
Company Policy & Personnel Book & Software Text Files	☐	☐	☐$ 89.95	☐$ 69.95		
Financial Management Techniques Book & Software	☐		☐$ 129.95	☐$ 119.95		
Start Your Business Paperback & Software (Software for Windows™)	☐			☐$ 24.95		
Successful Business Plan Book & Software for Windows™	☐		☐$125.95	☐$109.95		
Successful Business Plan Book & Software Templates	☐	☐	☐$109.95	☐$ 89.95		
BOOK & DISK PACKAGE TOTAL						

AUDIO CASSETTES

TITLE	Price	QUANTITY	COST
Power Marketing Tools For Small Business	☐ $ 49.95		
The Secrets To Buying & Selling A Business	☐ $ 49.95		
AUDIO CASSETTE SUB-TOTAL			

OASIS SUCCESS KITS   Call for more information about these products

TITLE	Price	QUANTITY	COST
Start-Up Success Kit	☐ $ 39.95		
Business At Home Success Kit	☐ $ 39.95		
Financial Management Success Kit	☐ $ 44.95		
Personnel Success Kit	☐ $ 44.95		
Marketing Success Kit	☐ $ 44.95		
OASIS SUCCESS KITS TOTAL			

COMBINED SUB-TOTAL (FROM THIS SIDE)

SOLD TO: *Please give street address*

NAME:
Title:
Company:
Street Address:
City/State/Zip:
Daytime Phone: Email:

YOUR GRAND TOTAL

SUB-TOTALS (from other side)	$
SUB-TOTALS (from this side)	$
SHIPPING (see chart below)	$
TOTAL ORDER	$

SHIP TO: *If different than above, please give alternate street address*

NAME:
Title:
Company:
Street Address:
City/State/Zip:
Daytime Phone:

If your purchase is:	Shipping costs within the USA:
$0 - $25	$5.00
$25.01 - $50	$6.00
$50.01 - $100	$7.00
$100.01 - $175	$9.00
$175.01 - $250	$13.00
$250.01 - $500	$18.00
$500.01+	4% of total merchandise

PAYMENT INFORMATION: *Rush service is available, call for details.*
International and Canadian Orders: Please call for quote on shipping.
☐ CHECK Enclosed payable to PSI Research   Charge: ☐ VISA   ☐ MASTERCARD   ☐ AMEX   ☐ DISCOVER

Card Number: Expires:
Signature: Name On Card:

Moonlighting 10/97